THE NEW SPEECH-O-GRAM TECHNIQUE FOR PERSUASIVE PUBLIC SPEAKING

C. RAYMOND VAN DUSEN, PH.D.

HOWARD VAN SMITH

THE NEW

SPEECH-O-GRAM

TECHNIQUE FOR

PERSUASIVE

PUBLIC SPEAKING

PRENTICE-HALL, INC.

ENGLEWOOD CLIFFS, NEW JERSEY

CONTENTS

1 THE METHOD

CHAPTER 1

WHERE ANGELS FEAR TO TREAD

IT HAPPENS MORE AND MORE.

You are sitting in an audience, innocently interested in what's going on, and then:

"Mr. Brown [Smith, Jones, or any name that might appear in the phone book], I wonder if you would give us your view on this matter . . . just a few words, you know."

Blame it on radio and TV, and audience participation shows, but today, if you want to be sure you will never be called upon to speak, you must stay away from all places where more than two or three people gather. It's no longer the exception; it's the rule—at least to the extent that you can't be certain someone won't say, "Mr. Brown, I wonder if . . ."

At the regular Thursday luncheon of a

civic group, one of the members turned to the newcomer next to him and advised him that he would be called upon to say a few words. It was a local custom, his neighbor told him with an easy smile. Nothing to it.

Now, this man was new in town and in business there. He was anxious to make a good appearance. But this ... local custom ... it came clear out of the blue—or out of a sky suddenly and ominously dark. He tried hard to think of something to say. In his excitement, ideas refused to come. He probed his brain for a joke to tell, although he already knew he was the serious type, not a funnyman. A picture of himself, bumbling and tongue-tied, began to form.

It wasn't as bad as that. Minutes later the chairman introduced him. A silence he felt was deadly followed as he got to his feet. Finally, looking down at his plate, he mumbled, "Uh ... I'm not much used to this ... but, well, I consider it an honor to be here with you people." A round of kindly and automatic applause followed. There was no real damage done.

But this man knew he had failed. This was the first chance, really, for those who would be his business associates to see and hear him. A time when he would be in such direct focus before all of them might never come again—and he had lost the opportunity to make good on that first impression by which people are so apt to judge.

He thought immediately afterward, once his excitement had eased off, of so much he could have said—words of such clarion sincerity that they would have produced just the effect he wanted. Why, he could have pointed out.... But what was the use now! And it could have been done so nicely. But this same thing is apt to happen when there is all the time in the world to prepare, and the cause—if you look closely—is still the same.

On another occasion a young man in business, who had caught his employer's eye, was asked if he would take over a speaking assignment. His audience was a group of businessmen, all identified with the same field. That narrowed down what he would say, and it gave them the label of experts.

Although he had a week in which to prepare, this young man was as much caught off guard as the newcomer at the civic luncheon. He felt he did his office job well (which was important!) and knew *that* was what had made the boss notice him. But as for public speaking . . . well, it was his boss, too, who had asked him to speak!

The young man was plainly frightened. Through seven troubled days and sleepless nights he worried about his talk and at times thought about possible ways he might get out of it. Finally, he decided to speak on "Window Dressing—or How the Public Sees Us." He jotted down some ideas he'd heard, some remembered from an old textbook, some that he now thought up, and on the seventh day, speech in pocket, approached the meeting as one walking solemnly to his doom. The waiting period while another man spoke heightened his fear. He saw his boss in the audience— and he'd thought he was there speaking because his boss couldn't attend! He recognized several business leaders in the field and decided they had forgotten more about "window dressing" than he'd ever know. Finally—in the midst of thoughts like these—he was called upon.

The young man delivered a speech. Like many a speech made by amateur speech-makers, it was filled with pauses that came out as "uhs," "ahs," "wells," and "I-meant-to-say's." It was a failure. He knew it. His boss knew it; the audience, including the local business leaders, knew it. It added nothing to the subject. It didn't help the prestige of the firm he represented. At the end, of course, everyone politely applauded. This speech was a perfect illustration of negation, representing the young man's attitude from the moment his boss asked him to make it.

Now let's analyze this a bit. Let's see where he went wrong, why he failed, why he—and his counterpart who bleated like a sick sheep at the civic luncheon—didn't have anything to say. The young businessman and the newcomer both felt insecure and fearful. This worked against them, froze them—but still we know the best speakers suffer this same kind of anguish.

There are no "born" speech-makers, really. Daniel Webster, the renowned orator who held audiences spellbound if ever anyone did, recalled his early attempts at speaking this way: "I could not speak before the school. Many a piece did I commit to memory and rehearse in my room over and over again, but when the day came and the master called my name and I saw all eyes upon me, I could not raise myself from my seat. When the occasion was over I went home and wept bitter tears of mortification."

Despite great handicaps other people have made remarkable successes on the speaking platform. For instance, a man with a stuttering problem is a popular after-dinner speaker. Others with impediments included Mrs. Eleanor Roosevelt, Sir Winston Churchill, and Charles Kingsley, the great novelist; it's a list that isn't hard to add to at all by calling to mind a lisp or other speech defect that has become an intimate part of some prominent person's manner.

But how is it done? It is true that a great speaker isn't made overnight, but a competent speaker—one whose talk will be admired, one who will make an audience happy to have spent time in listening to him—now can come into being in just a little more time than that.

The reason for that confident statement—at the moment still unqualified—is because shortly you will meet something entirely new, the Speech-O-Gram.

But first we must set a condition: you are not going to *read* your speech. The authors, who have listened to and dissected thousands of speeches, firmly believe that *reading* is not *speaking*. Freshness, intimacy, the very things that win an audience, are missing in a read speech. That does not mean that some prominent people cannot read their speeches effectively. They can, but only after rehearsals, coaching, and every device—such as the hidden prompter on TV—are conjoined to make the talk sound "off the cuff."

There's an old and rather sententious saying that sums this up: A free man speaks with his heart and a bound one with his lips. A recitation never has the *sound* of conviction. It has only the sound of recited words (and, in speaking before an audience, the additional crinkling of turned pages). That's not good enough. That's not speaking the way you really want to do it, anyway.

Now, if you're willing to bound over that hurdle with us, and if what you want is confidence, ease of manner, and that all-important something to say that will hold an audience's interest, you will get it. If you have already been asked to speak and you want answers on how to find the best subject, where to get material, how to put together a speech that will stay alive from start to finish—you will get that too. So let the Speech-O-Gram take over the worry.

With that decided, let's talk briefly about something called *pace,* the quality upon which the Speech-O-Gram is based. This benign ingredient, *pace,* is the "something" that gives a persuasive tone to a sell-out play, an absorbing book, a magazine article that isn't forgotten—and to a lot of other things that happen in public, including speaking. Some people call it *style,* others *handling* or *timing.* But by any name, it's the main difference between the entertaining pro and the dull—even though sometimes fervent— amateur.

The timing—perhaps not the style—was off for a little five-year-old girl who was attending dancing school. On a particular day the parents had been invited so that each youngster could show what she had learned. Just as the time came for the little girl to do her high-kicking number she made an important discovery and told the teacher, in effect, that she would have to sit this one out. Though beautifully dressed, she had left a very important ingredient at home—she had forgotten to wear her panties. In this instance, these were a necessity just as anecdotes, comparisons, jokes, quotes and simplified statistics are vital in successful speech making.

There is a striking similarity between a speech and a magazine article. Frequently, the difference is only that one is written and the other spoken. In plan of audience appeal, research and material selection—right up to the form of final delivery—they follow the same course. So let's lift out one sentence from a letter sent to a writer assigned to a story by Brooks Roberts, article editor of

This Week Magazine, whose weekly circulation of 14,000,000 is the largest in America. It is this: "Be sure to include plenty of anecdotes and quotes to illustrate the points you make."

That—the graphic impression—is the heart of the matter. It's the something recognized by every top comic, every leading playwright, anyone who has achieved the art of capturing an audience. Pace *isn't* an uphill charge at full tilt—that would only weary the audience which must try to keep up with it. It *is* like a series of waves, with moments of relief between each, that mounts to the final over-all effect. Pace is the difference between a persuasive and compelling speech and one that is tedious and boring—though both speakers start out with the same job to do.

But, you may say, achieving pace is an art that isn't easily come by. We agree. It is an art—but one that you may have immediately.

The authors decided that while a precise, easy-to-read treatment of public speaking would be helpful, its value would be limited. This viewpoint, oddly enough, was borne out by a high-ranking member of the Navy's public information office. He said his department, which sends out speakers, was entirely dissatisfied with ponderous tomes on the subject. He wanted a book that would steer a fast, exact course to a first-rate speech. The U. S. Navy, noted for direct action, didn't have time to spend on a lot of discursive theory.

But the writers wanted more than that. They wanted pace, too—the one way to be assured of a dud-proof speech.

The answer is the Speech-O-Gram. It goes with you to your assignment. It makes pace a certainty. You fill it in, timed for the length you want. It contains the facts and figures you cannot be expected to remember and the primary phrases that key you in to your audience. You are asked to recall only the anecdotes or stories, like the one about the little girl at dancing school. It has been found that those things which have a chronological or physical order cannot be forgotten even if you try, and that they may be easily narrated in their proper sequence. And, finally, the Speech-O-Gram looks like nothing more than the notes any speaker carries, in shuffle-proof form:

So relax. The rest is easy. Civilization, it is frequently recalled, wasn't able to get rolling until someone invented the wheel. We won't suggest that human progress and speech-making go hand in hand, because certainly some of the windy discoursers who have mounted the rostrum have reversed the direction of human progress instead. But for the job in hand you will find that the Speech-O-Gram is your "wheel."

You won't meet it until Chapter Five. In the meantime it will be necessary to get together on a few preliminaries, such as finding the key to your audience's interest and the material that will tune in to it. Then it will be time to put your speech together on the Speech-O-Gram, and you will see how all this will take care of itself.

CHAPTER **2**

CASING
YOUR
AUDIENCE

A WELL-KNOWN FOOTBALL COACH IN Michigan accepted an invitation to speak before a parent-teacher group at a local elementary school. He considered several topics to which his background would lend authority, then decided on "Touch Football for Tiny Toes." This was a subject about which he was entirely enthusiastic.

He built his speech around the advantages of supervised athletics for younger children, then larded it with anecdotes illustrating how early help had produced some of the game's greatest stars. He included a proposal for a long-range, fully organized program whose final effect would be to funnel talent to high-school and college teams. As a climax he painted graphic pictures of the exhibition games these flyweight teams would play, sponsored by fraternal organizations and given the color of "bowl" events.

In all, it was a well-designed speech delineating a plan to reach practically into the cradle to develop a future harvest of backs and linemen. This coach was an experienced speaker. He spoke lucidly, drawing from a rich fund of anecdotes of his background which illustrated the points he brought forward. (The ability to do a persuasive job on the platform is much more the rule than the exception among football coaches. In this profession, where the mortality rate caused by public and alumni opinion is high, it is necessary to win support by words as well as in stadiums. The late pudgy and amiable Herman Hickman became so liked as a speaker while head coach at Yale that he finally swapped careers, from coach to a highly paid commentator.)

The Michigan coach gave a spirited talk. As he went on he decided it was one of his best. Tonight he was especially fluent, forceful and stimulating. He didn't realize *how* stimulating until he sat down. The applause was scattered and only one robust male parent in the front row seemed fully enthusiastic. The program chairman asked if there were any questions. There were— many!

Half of the audience at once shot hands upward, but not out of curiosity. They arose, one by one, to object to any program like that, to put an end to it then and there before it was given a moment's consideration. They believed that children—their children!—in their early tender years should never be permitted to participate in contact sports because of possible lifelong injuries. Why, a short time before, a pediatrician had spoken to them on that very subject, and he'd had the support of the American Medical Association behind his every word.

This coach, who often had felt the tension his chosen work demanded, spent his most miserable half-hour fencing with an audience fully arrayed against him. It did not help that he knew that in a supervised sport the emphasis is placed first and foremost on how not to get injured; that it is the random, unorganized variety of the sport, in which kids indulge anyway, where they get their brains knocked out. He was caught in the full, swelling cry of public opinion, and there's no placating that.

but they might

Whatever thy hand finally to do it

with they might

Whatever thy hand findeth to do

do it with thy might

nothing ... between government

my ideals ... but doubt + fear,

anything ... doubt be between ... run

ideals but doubt + fear

power, power to convert to control

Mobil

MOBIL OIL CREDIT CORPORATION

SALESMAN	AUTO TAG NO.	STATE	DRIVERS LICENSE NO.	STATE

SOLD TO

TICKET NO.

MERCHANT

CUSTOMER COPY

X CUSTOMER SIGNATURE
NOT REQUIRED FOR
DEBIT CARD SALE

FCO-65 POS (8-84)

When he finally left the scene of this painful ordeal, he told himself he'd had it, and good! And he had no one else to blame but himself for not finding out in advance what these zealous protectors of youth were thinking and wanting to hear.

Now let's turn to a profession less honorable but one in which advance preparation is carried out to its most artful degree.

Burglars go about the job of surveying a situation systematically. They check on everything—the night watchman, the policeman walking the beat, the lighting, physiography, structural weaknesses that may be to their advantage—before they commit the robbery. They have what criminologists call a "modus operandi." It seems these crooks are really the ones who have appropriated as their slogan that old yet sage proverb, "Look ere thou leap!" They find this careful preparation necessary if they are to stay in business. It is called by their own colloquialism, "casing the joint."

If the coach had followed this procedure at least to some extent, he would have made vital discoveries and saved himself great embarrassment. He could easily have checked with the secretary of the group or the principal of the school. He could have asked about their interests and received helpful inside information. Then he could very wisely have suggested a number of subjects on which he was prepared to talk and have learned what the reaction would be. Definitely, he needed to "case the joint" before "pulling the job"!

Everyone who is about to give a speech needs all the information he can get about his audience's concerns, mood, problems, interests, age level, sex, occupations—and especially its particular likes and dislikes. Armed with this information, he can select his subject and anecdotes accordingly. He can decide whether his talk should be serious or light, formal or informal, entertaining, instructive, or inspirational. Without these facts, he may find himself before a group of strangers who will become more estranged each moment he talks.

This does not necessarily mean he cannot talk about the subject which is his foremost interest, that has his conviction behind it, the one in which his background and personal experience give him the self-assurance of his own authority. The approach to the subject, plus the way it is keyed to appeal by selection of anecdotes and material will always perform that part of the job notably.

Our friend the football coach, who left the auditorium muttering invectives at himself, knew well—though too late—that he could have met with high success if he'd switched his talk around to a sympathetic point of view, for instance, "How Scientific Football Guards Against Injury." He might even have had a fleet halfback sent up to him in the future by a parent who remembered his sane viewpoint.

An ancient bit of advice that is well accredited in these modern days of psychological insight is "Know thyself." To this might be added the counsel for every speaker: "Know thine audience before you say the first word." Woe may well and justly befall him who breaks this golden rule.

Another speaker, wiser in the ways of audiences, was asked to speak at a regional sales meeting of a large company which was about to introduce a revolutionary but scientifically sound idea. This company had stores all over the country, so that in addition to manufacturing the new commodity, it also had direct contact with the people who would buy it. First, the speaker had a talk with the regional director, during which the promotional problem was discussed. But even then he wasn't satisfied. He next went to one of the stores and spent some time "up front"—or at that all-important point where contact was made with the customer.

Armed with this information, he spoke on how to talk to the public when introducing a new but entirely sound idea—something that every businessman knows is always a ticklish problem to handle. He suggested a direct frontal attack and in keeping with this entitled his talk, "The Revolution—It's Here!" He brought out the objections that can be expected when any innovation in the normal structure of living is proposed, and told how to overcome them, through better understanding of human nature. An advertising man, he was eminently equipped to give advice of this sort.

So enthusiastically was his twenty-minute talk received, and so well was it aimed at his audience's interest, that copies of his speech were quickly printed and distributed to offices of the company throughout the nation. This man knew from his advertising background that an audience must be "felt" if it is to be reached. He had done a perfect job of "casing the joint."

The same is true of a woman who spoke before a state meeting of the PTA. on "Cheating Begins at Home." She first learned from the PTA. chapter at a local school that the organization was concerned with this problem and then gave it her novel slant.

It is always possible to question the chairman of the group, or the person who brings you the invitation to speak, on what your topic might be. But do not accept such an opinion as final. Better, let it help you find a slant of the problem on which you're best fitted to give helpful information. Experience shows that you won't meet opposition in doing this; in fact, such a slant, or more imaginative approach to the problem rather than a direct assault, usually makes the speech that really succeeds.

The word *"case"* can become a standard to help you survey your audience. Let each letter in the word serve as a reminder of the items to be checked:

C: Cares. What are the cares—problems, attitudes—of my prospective audience? Are they satisfied or dissatisfied with the way things are going? Do they have a problem which I can help solve?

A: Age. Will my audience consist of young people, middle-aged, older folk, or a mixture of all? Interests and attitudes vary greatly with age levels.

S: Sex. Will it be all male, all female, or both? Obviously, topics and anecdotes must change accordingly.

E: Enthusiasm. What are their chief interests? Do they like golf, bridge, football, knitting, club work, hot rods, psychological tinker-toys, market statistics, etc.? Are they businessmen who want to find new ways to increase sales, housewives with a keen interest in the home, men in the building trades concerned about community growth, students looking forward to a lifework?

What will be the C.A.S.E. of the group before which I will speak?

This information—an intimate understanding of these people—is the only way to begin a speech.

A professional magazine writer knows whether he is writing for a highbrow audience, a popular one, the men's field, home interest, or any of several others. He knows them all very well and succeeds because of this, while a multitude of others try and fail.

It isn't hard to find out. Perhaps a mere whirling of the telephone dial will provide the answer, or a luncheon meeting with someone in the group. In some instances it may take only a little thought and good judgment.

But be sure you always take this step: a good thoughtful pause before you start. Look across your desk and see for a moment these people before whom you will talk. If necessary, find out all there is to know about them.

Always C.A.S.E. your audience first.

CHAPTER 3

THE SOURCE
THAT
NEVER
FAILS

Aᴴ, ꜰɪɴᴇ!" ʏᴏᴜ ꜱᴀʏ. "ɴᴏᴡ ɪ ᴋɴᴏᴡ
how to find out exactly what my audience
will want to hear ... but how do I get the
material to do it?" In answer, let us recall
something we pointed out in the first chapter: in plan of production, a speech and
a magazine article are very much the same.
In getting material, the method is exactly
the same.

Perhaps, in keeping with a popular mis-
conception, you have thought that magazine writers are experts on the subjects on
which they write. You're right but in only
a few cases. Some are. They specialize in
crime, politics, outdoor life, agriculture,
and other subjects. Or, more rarely, they
may be experts or authorities because of
their background in one field; that is, they

23

are authorities who have turned to writing. (And yet we must add that even those in this enviable position must dig for fresh material at times.)

But most well-known magazine writers, such as A. E. Hotchner, Frank J. Taylor or Harold Martin, work the field in general. One of them may have just mailed a story to his editor on "How To Stop Cheating in Our Schools." His next may be "Emotion—a Traffic Killer!" It can vary even more than that—another might be on a recent medical discovery.

If the writer were to be his own source of material, for the first article he would need a degree in education or years of service as a teacher. For the second, he would have to combine the knowledge of a psychologist and a traffic engineer. For the third . . . well, a medical education takes at least seven years. Rather impossible, isn't it?

So how do these writers get their material—and how will you get yours?

There are three sources:

1. Your own background, especially if you are asked to speak on a subject because your experience is valuable.

2. Reference at the library.

3. Interviewing an authority, or authorities.

If you are in the enviable position of the expert and fit into class No. 1, your job often is fairly easy. Still, you will undoubtedly want to draw some new material from the other two sources. The exception to this is when you are asked to tell how you, your firm or organization, did something successfully.

But most speakers—and writers—work in No. 2. That means a trip to the library, usually the main branch if you are in a city where there are many. Ask immediately for the *Reader's Guide to Periodic Literature*. This will tell you what has been written on the subject back to the turn of the century. (There's another guide covering the nineteenth century, if for some reason you want to go back into that period.) It's a good idea to use a little discretion and not try to cover everything that comes under the heading. From the descriptions of the articles, you can make a fairly accurate choice. Never fear that you won't get enough material. Your next step should be to ask the reference department for the back numbers in which these articles appeared.

The reference department of a library is always most helpful. It has been our experience, and that of many others who make use of this wonderful source of material, that reference librarians will go to extremes to help you. If you tell the person to whom you speak exactly what you are doing, he will probably direct you, as an expert in such research, to a source of information you would otherwise not find. Here you can also inquire about books on your subject, if you feel you have need of more material.

The third source, the interview, is the best way to get new, fresh material. It's rather unnecessary to say that this "something extra" you've shown the initiative to go out and get will add considerably to the effect of your speech.

Does the thought of calling up a big name and asking for a short interview frighten you? Don't let it. Perhaps because it tickles their egos, these people usually are not only willing but also extremely pleasant about it. Tell the authority you pick exactly why you want to interview him. Then carry to the interview with you, in the back of your mind, a few good, challenging questions to ask.

One young speaker unexpectedly turned his first speech into a notable event this way. He questioned a scientist of high repute in electronics about future developments. His speech not only went off well but got six paragraphs in the morning paper, after the scientist had confirmed what the young speaker had said.

Now let's make a very pertinent point. Whether you use one of these sources, or two, or all three combined, remember you do not want only dry facts. You also must have examples of how someone did this or that of which you're talking, why they succeeded or failed. In using quotes be sure you give credit where credit is due—an honorable rule when using material from various sources.

For each statement, each fact, each recitation of a definite result, try whenever possible to find an example or anecdote to illustrate it. These little illustrative stories are the heart of the matter, the way to achieve that all-important quality called *pace*. You can bore an audience to death with the best set of facts ever put together; but you can keep them high in their seats with the refreshing pause of anecdotes spaced so as to let them see how it all happened. That's the material you must put into your notes now as you research your job. It means, really, going always from the abstract back to the world of people and movement, to life as we know and understand it. It means that there's something like a movie screen in the minds of your hearers that you must keep alive or the screen and their brains will go dim.

This is the material you need for the graphic impression, which is the *raison d'être* of the Speech-O-Gram, and you're only one chapter away from it now.

CHAPTER 4

THE
FOOLPROOF
SPEECH

A QUICK STUDY OF A SELECTED SPEECH that has been fully audience-tested and found foolproof will help you understand the little things, the parts which joined together make a speech go.

The one we've chosen isn't the best ever given, but still it is sound and serviceable; it fits the needs of nearly any group. It won't make you a William Jennings Bryan, a Chauncey Depew or a Bennett Cerf, but it will make you an adequate speaker. By that we mean it's a speech you couldn't very well slip on. As such, it's a good speech to study, part by part. The criterion being that it could be adapted for use before just about any audience, we'll let it stand without identification.

This talk lasted within a few seconds of twenty minutes, a time that's neither impolitely short nor wearily long. In fact, in general it is an uncommonly good length.

The subject is public relations, which is key-point number one in its widespread interest and adaptability. Public relations is important to any group today, for to succeed in this modern world in silence is next to impossible. The present time has been called everything from the jet and atomic age to the neurotic age. Though it may be characterized as any of these, it is also the outspoken advertising age, advertising and publicity being the advance guard of all activity.

You have to sell whatever you propose. Every group knows it has this problem—we defy you to find one that isn't interested in this kind of helpful information. You can include women's clubs, the Exchangites, Kiwanians, Optimists, Rotarians, PTA, Woodmen of the World, the Red Cross, even the Boy Scouts. For everyone— everyone!—needs public support.

Can you possibly go wrong with a subject like that?

On the following pages about one third of this speech is given. That is, we've stripped it down to its mechanics to show how it was put together. These pieces—a little on the abrupt and discordant side when taken out of context—are the keys to how the speech was constructed.

The brief comments at the right take you behind the scenes of the speech in order to show you the ropes that make the curtains go up and down and the control board that adjusts the lights.

Some of the terms denoting the structural parts of the speech are the ones you will meet in the next chapter on the Speech-O-Gram. You haven't seen them before, but they are the same language the Marine Corps uses to describe the phases of a campaign. Speakers, the same as Marines, have an objective to take.

MEETING THE PUBLIC AT SIDEWALK LEVEL

(*This title, which chairman will use to introduce the speaker, primes audience's interest*)

Mrs. Roberts, your chairman, has told me one of your biggest problems is a job that would seem the easiest in the world—

Scoop opener ties in with audience's problem

giving away money. That's the reason I decided to talk on Meeting the Public at Sidewalk Level. You might say that you and I are both commanded by this generous spirit. You see, I'm in banking. (. . . .)

This occasion brings to mind an event widely publicized a few years back. You'll recall the details—the man who tried to sell brand-new one-dollar bills at a discount on the streets of a large city and got no takers.

Jump-off story serves as quick starter

Passers-by were skeptical, thought there was a "catch." Everyone knows there is no "catch" in Social Security, just as there is no "catch" in good United States currency, but people—we know—need educating. Many are unaware of the "assists" that are commonplace to you and me. (. . . .)

This paragraph helps crystallize problem for audience

If you will let me, it is my idea tonight to suggest ways and means of accomplishing this task. (. . . .)

Speaker boldly states purpose

The first consideration in doing this will be the humane side, with stress on kindness in the treatment of others.

Objectives are given briefly

The all-important human side will be discussed and two important obstacles—brevity of attention span and fixed personal habits—pointed out.

Final consideration will be the various communicative media and how to use them in accomplishing your job.

Application of these principles will lighten your burden, get better results, improve your efficiency and effectiveness. (. . . .)

Speaker makes a promise

First, it must be remembered that how we treat other people reflects on our own character, also on our employer. Every one of us is a public relations representative of the organization that employs us and this determines our own success as well as the success of our employer. When I first came to this town, I was looking about for a neighborhood store with which to do business. I met with a very haughty attitude at the first place I stopped. I pulled my tail under my legs and left. In another store down the street, I felt welcome and at home immediately. I was greeted by friendly faces. (....)

Advance starts. First objective is illustrated by personal experience

No matter what we are doing, we must work with people. Success always includes the human element because people are the substructure of any private or public enterprise. Successful people understand their fellow man. As Carlyle said, "A great man shows his greatness by the way he handles men." (....)

Advance continues and is backed up with quote

One of our great industrial leaders relates that as a boy he carried newspapers in a large box fastened to a sled. Along the route, youngsters would gather around and he was afraid of what might happen to his merchandise. At first, he didn't know how to handle the situation. Finally, a good idea struck. He looked over the lot and tried to pick a good leader, the biggest of the crowd. Then he said, "Will you take charge here?" That boy saw to it that nothing happened to the sled or papers because he had status in the group now. The newsboy had used

Story furthers this idea

a very practical approach to handling
people. (....)

People want to maintain their feeling of
self-importance. They don't want to be
shoved around like sacks of wheat at a
granary. (....)

The thought is
amplified

Few people are like Si Hodges who had
the reputation of being the laziest man
in town. When asked by a farmer if he
would like to help with the harvest, Si
asked, "How much will yuh pay me?"
"I'll pay you what you're worth," replied
the farmer. Si pondered for a moment,
then answered, "I'll be durned if I'd ever
work for that." (....)

Humorous story
furthers this
idea

Your desire to be humane in your treatment of human beings is a policy that
should be furthered by every employee
in your organization. Human understanding is the oil that keeps the ma-
chinery working in perfect harmony.
(....)

Brief recap
given to cover
first objective

You are dealing with human beings as
you work at "sidewalk level" and you
must remember their strengths and weaknesses. I consider their desire to be
treated as individuals as a strength. The
second but not less important consideration is the human side which includes
such weaknesses as: brevity of attention
span and fixed habit patterns. These are
human factors.

This paragraph
serves as a bridge
and designates
second objective,
also gives quick
rundown on what
is to follow

The attention span is brief. People con-
centrate for only short periods. Look at
the outline of this box for a few moments.

First obstacle
pointed out and
illustrated

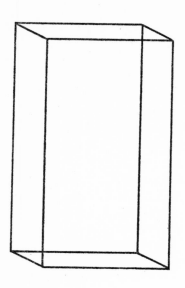

This visual, drawn on a 10" by 16" card, is held up in front of audience for 30 seconds

At first, you see it in one perspective. Then it changes form and you see a different picture. Attention is a great deal like that visual image. It comes and goes. Unless we have disciplined ourselves, our attention shifts quickly from one subject to another. We learn vital lessons from this weakness of human nature. The stimulus we present must be strong, vivid, with clear-cut lines, and it must be presented many times. (....)

Illustration is discussed

People are victims of habit. They're like the man who was being discussed by two young ladies. One remarked, "Oh, he is so romantic. When he speaks to me, he calls me 'Fair Lady.'" "Force of habit, my dear. He's a railroad conductor." Old people get into grooves. It's almost impossible to show them anything new. If

Second obstacle introduced. Illustrative story backs it up

we erect signs on the edge of the grooves, they do not see them. They don't stick their heads up that far. We've got to make them run into the message face to face. (....)

Your answer to this problem is enlightenment—enlightenment of your own personnel and the public. You must find or devise means of reaching out through the various media of communication with a loud, clear voice and understandable words. (....)

Speaker develops third objective

You have many public interest stories to illustrate this. What about the story I heard one of your workers tell of the distressed seventy-two-year-old widow who did not know that her security had been provided because her deceased husband had had a Social Security card? (....)

He tells them what materials to use, illustrates with a story

But the program must be slanted to suit each particular area. Methods with rural areas must be different from those used in urban areas, and never underestimate the farmer. Several years ago I saw a prize Jersey heifer grazing on a Vermont hillside. I drove around the hill to the farmer's home and asked the man how much he would take for the cow. He scratched his head for a second, and then said, "Now, look-a-here, be you the tax assessor, or has she been killed by the railroad?" (....)

He develops previous idea and spells it out with a personal experience story

Radio and TV utilize some useful techniques that you might find helpful in your educational program. Just last night I watched a panel where (....)

A specific suggestion is made

On his deathbed Governor Hogg of Texas requested that no monument be placed at his grave; but that instead,

Assault starts with story

there be planted "at my head a pecan tree, and at my feet an old-fashioned walnut, and when these trees shall bear, let the pecans and walnuts be given out among the Plains people of Texas, so that they may plant them and make Texas a land of trees."

His wishes were carried out. The first nuts were saved in 1926 and planted in nursery rows. The same thing has been done each year since. When the saplings are large enough to transplant they are distributed to schools and county boards.

Each time you are similarly generous and kind, you help others and plant seeds of good will for your bureau. The wrong kind of treatment results in perverse attitudes, the "deaf ear," the "closed mind," whereas the right kind results in cooperation and helpfulness. Obviously, your load is lightened and everyone profits when you are humane. (. . . .)

Gains from first objective shown

A taxi driver in St. Louis was telling me about his job. "It's not the work I enjoy," he said in all seriousness, "it's the people I run into."

Story leads into gains from second objective

People are wonderful when you understand them, accept their weaknesses, cease to deal with them blindly. When you have difficulty communicating with them and your knowledge of psychology tells you that they listen for only short periods and seldom veer in their way of doing things, then you develop patience. Feelings of frustration disappear, you come to enjoy your work, and your techniques improve. (. . . .)

The son of an Iowa farmer had never spoken, but one day in his fourteenth year he saw a bull charging his father from the rear. Without a second's hesitation, he yelled, "Look out, Dad, that bull is a-gonna horn you!" The father was amazed and after a successful escape remarked to the boy, "You said that as clear as anything. Why is it you didn't speak before?" "Wal," admitted the son, "guess it was because I didn't have anything important to say."

Story leads into gain from third objective

You realize that you have many important things to say to many people all the time, and you know that you can't get your message across without the help of the giant voices of radio, TV, and the newspapers. (....)

Your effective use of these media pays off in public enlightenment so that you don't have to do the job piecemeal. Certainly, it relieves you of a heavy burden.

Gain is shown

The greatest value of the humane treatment, human understanding, and the use of mass communication media is that it makes your job easier. That's what's in it for you.

Brief statement shows what listener gets out of it

In closing, let me remind you that people want to be treated as thinking individuals—not as one of a mass. We must recognize their differences. (....)

The Mop-up starts; the speaker is summarizing his main points

Secondly, we must know the people we are trying to educate—their weaknesses and their strengths. (....)

Thirdly, we need to learn to express ourselves clearly and use specific, direct appeals. (....)

Last, we must use as many communicative media as possible to get facts across to the people. (....)

If we are going to succeed, we must be human and recognize human weaknesses. Charles Lamb said once, "Don't introduce me to that man! I want to go on hating him and I can't hate a man whom I know." If, in our dealings with human beings, we are to be successful, we must know people. And through knowing them, we must come to understand them and let them know that we realize we are one of them. Doing it this way, your job is made easy.

Mop-up completed, speaker closes on serious note

CHAPTER 5

MEET
THE
SPEECH-O-GRAM

Some People Make Too Big a Chore of speech preparation: they pore through long books; make no end of notes; write and rewrite their opus many times. Their brains and paper are cluttered with useless material and later they have trouble sorting out key points and illustrative stories. This cumbersome approach results in confusion and heavy speeches.

An old German proverb holds when there is a speech to prepare: "The best carpenters make the fewest chips."

On such streamlined philosophy the Speech-O-Gram is based. It is a fast-moving vehicle with sleek lines, the opposite of the junk dealer's pushcart with its jumbled mass of odds and ends, most of which should be thrown away because they have no usefulness. The goal, as we have said before, is pace.

The Speech-O-Gram, then, is a self-organizing device designed for pace. The result is a light load that's easy to take, with pertinent pieces in proper places and no lost time—either for you or the audience.

The first step is the "Scoop," which in Marine parlance means the plan of campaign. Your audience is told, first, what you are going to say and why. Then your words are held in the focus you want them. That's the proper way and only way to begin a speech, immediately letting the fiddlers and tweedlers out in advance. It amounts to a forthright statement of purpose, an honest declaration of intention. No fooling around!

The "Jump-Off" is next. It sets the stage completely, all characters in place. Here the speaker tells the points or objectives he will make so that the audience knows exactly what he will cover. This is the place for an explanation to the ever-present but unasked question: "What's in this for me (or my organization)?"

In the "Advance" you bring out the highlights. Now is the time to be logical and drive through with all the arguments and persuasive material you have gathered.

The "Assault" phase follows. The tempo is swift. This is the high point of your speech, so hit hard and fast! It's the place you've saved for selling the most doubtful skeptic in your audience. It's the climax.

The "Mop-Up" is short, restates concisely the principal points of your talk, nails them down, sums up what you've said. Here you do not dwaddle, adding forgotten details or inserting new material that comes to mind. Never! But it is the place to throw in a final punch-line of encouragement that might spark future action.

The over-all pace is planned, a great deal like the three acts of a play. The "Scoop" and "Mop-Up" correspond to the prologue and epilogue.

Abraham Lincoln said, "Be sincere, be simple, be seated." Add this wonderful quality of sincerity as best you can and begin following the Speech-O-Gram as it is given on the following pages. This one has been filled out as the speaker who talked on "Meeting the Public at Sidewalk Level" would have used it.

SPEECH-O-GRAM

place: Social Security League
time: 8:30 p.m.   date: 4/18/58

title: MEETING THE PUBLIC AT SIDEWALK LEVEL

Time
(min.)

SCOOP: Mrs. Roberts, your chairman, has told me one of your biggest problems is a job that would seem the easiest in the world — giving away money. That's why I decided to talk on Meeting the Public at Sidewalk Level. You might say you and I are both commanded by this generous spirit. You see, I'm in banking.

JUMP-OFF: Brings to mind the story of selling dollar bills — passer-by thought there was a "catch."

1   If you let me, I'll suggest ways and means of accomplishing this task.
Objective A: First consideration is the humane side.
Objective B: The all-important human side, the obstacles.
Objective C: The various communicative media — how to use them.
Promise: Application of these principles will lighten your burden, get better results, improve your efficiency and effec-
2   tiveness.

ADVANCE: How we treat others reflects on our own character. Everyone a public relations representative of organization he works for. Determines our and employer's success.

3 Story: Personal experience in locating neighborhood store.

No matter what we are doing, must work with
4 others. People the substructure of private and public enterprise. Quote Carlyle, "A great man shows his greatness by the way he handles people."

5 Story: Industrial leader once a newsboy. People want to feel self-important — don't want to be pushed around.

6 Story: Si Hodges, "I'll be durned if I'll work for that." Every employee should further humane attitude (oil).

7 You deal with human beings at "sidewalk level" — remember strengths and weaknesses. Desire to be treated as individuals a strength.

8 Second consideration, the human side — includes weaknesses; short attention span; fixed habits. Attention span is brief, concentration period short. (Show visual, describe.) Perspective changes. Attention, like that
9 visual image, comes and goes. Must make stimulus strong. Story: People are victims of habit — like the two ladies discussing a man.

10 Old people get into grooves — must meet message face to face. Enlightenment the answer — TV, radio. Story: Tell public interest stories — 72-year-old distressed widow.

11 Suit programs to area — rural, urban. Story: Never underestimate farmer-type Jersey. Radio, TV, offer helpful techniques (TV panel).

12   ASSAULT: Gov. Hogg requested no monument at grave, "at my head a pecan tree, and at my feet a walnut."

     Each time you are generous and kind, plant
13   seeds of good will for bureau. Wrong treatment results in perverse attitudes, "deaf ear," "closed mind." Right kind, cooperation, helpfulness. Result, your load is lightened.

14   Story: St. Louis taxi driver, "It's not the work I enjoy, it's the people I run into." People are wonderful when you understand them, accept their weaknesses, cease to deal with them blindly.

15   When communication is difficult and your knowledge of psychology tells you they listen for short periods, show new ways, patience and enjoyment of work comes.

16   Story: Iowa farmer's son had never spoken, bull charges father, "Look out, Dad..."

     You realize you have many important things
17   to say to many people. Need help of TV, radio, newspapers. Use enlightens public, relieves you of heavy burden.

     Greater value of humane treatment, human understanding, use of media — makes your job easier.

18   MOP-UP: In closing, let me remind you that people want to be treated kindly, as individuals. Must know their strengths and weaknesses. Need to express yourselves
19   clearly, use specific direct appeals. Quote Charles Lamb, "Don't introduce me to that man! I want to go on hating him and I can't hate a man whom I know," To be successful you must know people, understand them, let them know you realize you are one of them.
20   Doing it this way, your job is made easy.

6

THE

SCOOP

IN NEWSPAPER PARLANCE, THE REPORTER who gets there first with an important story has "scooped" the other boys. If he can do this often enough, he stands a good chance of a raise because his stuff pulls extra reader interest. The speaker who can do the same with his talk has the edge too— and in more ways than one.

Material and a title that are new and different arouse audience curiosity in the fastest way possible—by making people want to be there to be in on "scoop" news too.

At a state convention of bankers in Chicago several meetings were being held simultaneously. Most of the members jammed into one hall; the other speakers had only a sprinkling attending their talks. The heavy rain of listeners overflowed the hall where the announced subject was "Ten New Tellers in Ten Months . . . Why?" The speaker followed through on this by giving the inside story of his bank's rapid growth and told of the ideas and devices that had helped bring this about.

If you were a banker and had been at this convention, it's rather safe to assume that this would have been the talk you would have gone to hear. The idea nearly dares you not to. This man started in the right place—with an ingenious title. Then he gave a speech that fulfilled the promise. And the result, to borrow an expression from the stage, was "good show!"

But suppose you are asked to give a speech and find yourself in the position of an outsider looking in. Here's what one ingenious speaker did. Though he was neither salesman nor insurance man, through one of those odd miscastings of fate he was asked to talk at a regional meeting of a group of insurance salesmen. Knowing little about the subject, he hit upon the idea of telling them what he and other laymen didn't like about the attitudes and approaches of insurance salesmen. His title: "Your Mirror Talks Back."

He complimented them on some recent improvements in technique, but kidded them, too, about some present pressure tactics. He had them laughing at themselves (once they saw themselves from the customer's side), while he suggested ways to improve their "cudgeling" by use of a "soft" approach. His talk was a booming success. It got more response than did the speeches of the specialists in the field because it was novel, fresh and helpful. And it was information that couldn't have come from an expert, at least with such intimate freshness. It was "scoop" all the way.

Similarly, a layman speaking on a panel in which nursing education was discussed used somewhat the same idea. He called his talk "The Patient's Viewpoint." He admitted little knowledge of the subject, then went on to suggest that the group get information from patients on what nurses should know, rather than sit around and theorize about it. The professional people had not considered this new angle before and listened intently, later deciding to prepare a questionnaire for such a study.

Here again, an unusual suggestion produced a favorable response and prompted action on the part of the listeners. There is no better test of the success of a speech.

This man and the speaker at the insurance convention certainly had perfect excuses to utter an emphatic No! when asked to speak. But they accepted the challenge of speaking under a handicap and came up with "diamond studs" because they had originality and a good sense for "scoop treatment."

Instead of going about the assignment in the hard way—boning up on what the experts already knew, and trying to learn a subject fully without time to do it—they used their own personal experiences, consequently making preparation an easy task. And, too, the titles these two men used should be noticed, because titles set the tenor of a speech in advance. A speech has got to start somewhere and frequently a title, if it's a good and stimulating one, is just the place to begin. While this can't be called a rule, it is called a good idea. If you start off high, you're only apt to end that way.

Here's another case of "scoop" tied in with personal experience. A young assistant magazine editor was hurriedly called upon to speak before a college class in article writing, when a scheduled speaker was unable to appear. He had only a few hours to prepare. He decided (because there was no time to "research" an important treatment of his subject) just to talk easily on what he thought his audience would like most to hear. The result combined "scoop," personal experience, and a masterful use of psychology.

He asked only one question: "How many people will be there?" He took with him enough copies of a recent issue of the magazine he worked for so that each listener would have one. His subject: "Why We Print the Kind of Stories We Do."

Even with so little time for planning, this speech became one of the most successful ever given—though the young man had never thought of himself as a speaker. He gave them an inside story, keyed to their prime interest, and one they couldn't get elsewhere. It was authentically part of his own experience; he was the speaking proof of what he said. While he was talking, his audience was busy not in gaping at him but in turning the pages as he went from story to story. That was the touch of psychology.

In his talk he explained the reason the editors had selected each story. This was vital, inside information—working information to a class in article writing. Except for a few words needed to open and close, the magazine pages served as his "outline." This speaker has since been asked to come back each year and the request is always the same: "Give it exactly the same way again. They eat it up." It is also interesting to note that somewhere along the line the "expert" speaker he replaced the first time was entirely forgotten.

It can be said that the speaker who knows his speech is unusual, different, exciting, a "scoop," is like the giver of a well-selected Christmas gift: he wants to give it. Such a feeling quickly dispels concern about success on the platform. Eagerness about subject matter can cause the speaker to forget the pins and needles that prick his nervous system. He wants to get to the platform with it, once it is prepared.

Such preparation is not difficult if you are willing to allot some time for idea gathering. If you know something about your prospective audience and the occasion, and a good idea does not pop up of its own accord—then it's time to go idea shopping. We have already discussed how to "case" the audience and where to get material. What we are doing now is a little different. Now is the time to think about the angle you'll adopt in presenting your subject. Give this much thought because it is all-important. Look at your subject matter from one side and then the other, always with that audience in mind. Then when you've got it, boil the idea down to capsule size. That's your title.

Put it at the top of your Speech-O-Gram and you're under way.

QUICK-STARTERS

Someone has said, "If you don't strike oil in the first three minutes, quit boring." This is a good maxim for public speakers, but the time—three minutes—is too long. You need to get the audience interest within the first minute. The best way to do this is with what is sometimes called a "quick-starter."

An incidental story (which is about the easiest thing in the world to tell) that gives a good strong clue to your speech content, does this very nicely for you. It is the natural way to lead in, and people always enjoy this personal way of talking. Win them then and they're apt to be with you all the way through. We strongly advise this type of opener, at least for the first go-round.

One of the most succesful speakers we know always finds something in the immediate situation that fills this part of the bill. Usually he makes one of the following his first sentence:

"As I entered the auditorium tonight, Harry Blank asked me . . ."

"Just as I was leaving home to come over to talk with you, my wife told me . . ."

"Mrs. John Blair, whom you all know well, was telling me about some of the problems you ladies are facing in this club. As a result, I have decided to talk on . . ."

These on-the-spot interest rousers have always served that speaker well as starters. Audiences like them because of their warmth and hominess. Listeners like to know that the speaker is one with them, and such suggestions of personal contact serve to bind audience and speaker together.

Your job as a speaker is twofold: (1) to tell your audience what you will talk about and (2) to form a bond with them by showing that you understand what they are trying to do.

Another way of opening (but if this is your first speech you may want to pass up this method for the present because it takes more self-assurance in the handling) is the straight story, light or fully serious. Here you start with an incident or anecdote seemingly foreign to the ocasion, but which leads adroitly to the subject of the speech.

An example of such a story—this time on the light side—is the one told of James M. Barrie when he addressed a thousand girls at Smith College during a visit to America. A friend asked him how he enjoyed the experience. "Well," said the great playwright, "to tell the truth, I'd rather talk one thousand times to one girl than talk one time to a thousand girls."

Another way of opening is the appropriate quotation, though we might as well warn you here that this can often come out with a stiff and overly formal sound that might not help you along in establishing that bond with your audience. Quotes, like anecdotes, come by the volume, or you can often find them sprinkled throughout your daily paper if you read with an eye open for them.

Now—what about jokes? This may surprise you, but we are seriously inclined to answer this way:

Jokes aren't funny.

A sports writer in Miami, who had been asked to address the Rotary Club there, asked several people in the city room of his newspaper if they knew a good funny story with which he might begin his talk. Someone told him a hilarious one about a midget, and the sports writer set out happily with a story guaranteed to lay them in the aisles. Except—as he got up to talk, he noticed two very short men sitting directly in front of him. He was suddenly bereft of a "spot" story.

On another occasion—and there are so many of these happenings we could fill pages with them—a speaker opened up with a joke about a man with a glass eye. Afterward, someone told him that the chairman who had introduced him possessed just that sort of eye.

But the main reason for not using jokes is that telling funny stories is a separate art. If your joke goes flat, which it might, your confidence may go flat with it.

Jackie Gleason, Bob Hope, Red Skelton, Groucho Marx, and all the others have worked for years perfecting their joke-telling techniques. And yet even these experts, with their writing staffs and years of experience, come up with occasional dead fish. Why should the once-a-month speaker assume that he'll be able to "wow" them with a sidesplitter he picked up in the barbershop or the locker room?

Now let's recapitulate on these various quick-starters:

1. Incidental story which shows your interest in their problem.

2. Straight story which leads indirectly into problem.

3. Quotation pertinent to occasion.

4. Joke.

Our advice on which one to use is exactly the same as the way they are numbered. Of course, you can nicely and effectively join two of these: the incidental story with one or the other following as an illustration, or an anecdote of any kind which will serve that purpose.

CHAPTER 7

JUMP-
OFF

SHAKESPEARE, IN HIS PLAY *Much Ado About Nothing*, paid a man high praise. He said, "He was want to speak plain and to the purpose." As a public speaker, you too will be highly complimented if your audience says the same of you. But you've got to make it so.

Once you've decided on your Scoop subject, you need to ask yourself two questions: "What is my purpose in giving this speech? What do I expect to accomplish?"

As we've said before, important factors determining the target you set for yourself will include: your audience, their interests, the situation, and the subject. If you know they have a problem, your purpose in speaking may be to help them solve it. The sample speech, "Meeting the Public at Sidewalk Level," did just that. The statement of purpose was phrased as follows: "... it is my purpose tonight to suggest ways and means of accomplishing this task."

Most any problem-solving statement of purpose can be put in somewhat the same way. Another model might be, "I want to show how, with a little effort, you can . . ."

However, not every speech follows this formula. The simple statement, "My purpose in speaking on this subject is to show that . . ." is suited to a talk that is meant to instruct the audience. If you want to impress them, a more apt staement might be, "The discussion of this subject should make us all realize that . . ." The talk that attempts to get action may include a definite proposal such as, "After you have heard this, I'm sure you will decide that you should . . ."

So it goes. Suit the statement of purpose to the audience, their interests, the situation and your subject. By speaking out plainly at the beginning you make certain there will be no doubt about what you are intending to say. Throughout, the audience knows where you stand and everything about your talk is related to that. This part of your speech should stand out definitely, in simple language, with clear-cut lines. It's the time, as they say, to call a spade a spade. Fancy language will only blur the effect.

It's the time to *zero in* on your target.

Put it just that way to open the Jump-Off section of the Speech-O-Gram.

NAME YOUR OBJECTIVES

There's a maxim frequently used in public speaking which advises the speaker to "tell 'em what you're going to tell 'em, then tell 'em what you've told 'em." In this part of the Jump-Off, in which you cover the specific objectives of your talk, you "tell 'em what you're going to tell 'em."

Actually, you present an ungarnished outline of the main points of your speech, putting it in simple, logical order. Without details! In the Advance which follows you will develop those points.

Having stated your purpose, you may say, "This discussion will include consideration of . . . and . . ."; "Vital points to consider in this matter . . ."; or "I will discuss the following points . . . First . . . Second . . . Third . . ."

Now, having set down your outline, you have ordered yourself to stay with it, never rambling off on some irrelevant phase or throwing in foreign material that has no direct bearing. This is the part of the talk that compares to the train caller's announcement of stops along the way. You know what he says: "Chiiiicaaaggoo train leaving on track ten, stops at Buuufffaaallo, Tooolllleeedo, Elllkkkkkarrr, Gaaayyyreee, and Chiiiicaaaaggoo." You do the same in your objectives, the part of a speech which some call the run-down.

The newly elected Tail Twister (he's the man who places devious fines on members and makes the collections during luncheon meetings) in a Los Angeles Lion's Club was required to give a speech upon his acceptance of his post. When he got to his objectives, he said, "I have three important points to make in my speech today. First, I will carry out my assignment with diligence so the club will profit. Second, the club will profit because of my diligence. Third, I'm going to fine the hell out of you!"

Another good example was contained in the speech of a lady talking to a Cleveland Women's Club on the subject "Hospitality at Home." In this phase of the speech she said, "My discussion includes three vital points: codes for the host; the hostess, amenities and duties; and children at adult social functions."

These statements of the objectives are clear-cut and indicate exactly what the speaker intends to cover in his talk. Although it lasts for only one, two, or three sentences, it is an all-important part of the speech. It orients the audience; that is, it lines up their thinking for the best reception of the subject.

Said Shakespeare, "Brevity is the soul of wit." Use brevity here. In this part of your speech "don't write—telegraph!" Say it in as few words as possible, then stick to your promise and stay with the points as you've outlined them. Make them quickly, logically, in one, two, or three sentences, and put them in telegraphic English. Write them that way where the objectives are listed in the Jump-Off section of the Speech-O-Gram.

WHAT'S IN IT FOR ME?

A motorist who had bogged down in the sticky red clay of an unpaved Georgia road had just paid a Georgia cracker $10 to be pulled out with a team of mules.

"I should think," said the motorist, as he got back into his car, "that you would be pulling people out of this stuff day and night."

"Nope," drawled the mule driver, "at night's when we tote the water for the roads."

Consciously or unconsciously, listeners are like the Georgian; they are looking at the speech from the what's-in-it-for-me standpoint. They want to know how the talk will help them. You, the speechmaker, would be wise to ask yourself early, "What will this talk do for my audience?" Once you've decided, write it into the Speech-O-Gram at the end of the Jump-Off.

Certainly, what you say is going to do something for them: Give them new information; help them solve problems; help them to make a decision or formulate a point of view; show them how to do something more easily, efficiently, appropriately. In one way or another, you're out to help them.

A brief statement of the value of this talk to the audience helps greatly to accomplish the purpose of holding attention. Your speech might easily start off with a bang and get interest immediately; but it might soon lose its effectiveness because what you say has a doubtful personal value to the listeners, now that they've had time to mull over in their minds the idea of your talk. You're about to start the Advance now, and you must have their full interest.

So tell them. Make the promise that what you are going to say is essential to their problem.

This also works in another way. It is a direct challenge to you now as you put your points down on paper. Once you write it into your Speech-O-Gram, it is like your conscience, constantly before you, urging you to keep your word. You have no right to stray.

A speaker talking to a Tacoma, Washington, group of school daddies said at this point, that he would tell them how they could ascertain the educational potentials of their children; how far they could be expected to go, whether they had a genius or two on their hands. His what's-in-it-for-me promise was stated as follows: "The information I am about to give you tonight will show you fathers how you can find out what your children's mental powers are, and how much they should be expected to attain through education." He had their interest primed. Then, in the Advance, he described reliable tests that the youngsters could take which would predict their future possibilities. He named the tests, telling the fathers where they could go to have the study made. The audience of dutiful daddies listened attentively; they wanted this information, every word of it—and naturally the speech was a success. The speaker had kept the promise he made in the Jump-Off.

After that speech, many of the parents took their children to a nearby university guidance center for testing, proving beyond doubt that his speech had come off successfully.

A speech that can stir such action certainly can be called successful, and that is what you should always try for: a definite response by getting your audience to do something, feel something, take a new turn. When you accomplish this, there was something in it for them.

But it all begins with that promise. It's your guide from now on.

Write it in your Speech-O-Gram. You've said it and you mean it. Now you'll show them you do.

CHAPTER 8

THE
ADVANCE

Now THE ADVANCE STARTS. YOU MADE a path for yourself when you listed your objectives. Now it is up to you to follow that path.

Move to your first point immediately—just as you gave it as your first objective—and develop it.

One of the best ways to do this is to make a statement, present some figures, or anything that could be called "startling." That doesn't mean you are expected to shock people out of their chairs; rather, just joggle their attention a bit by what you say. A good illustrative story might best do this, but whatever it is, the effect you're out to achieve is always the same.

It might be wise to toss in here an important warning about figures. Figures, if cautiously used, are very helpful with most audiences. If used in generous amounts, running into heavy statistics, they will produce about the same result as nembutal or any other good sleeping pill.

One simple statement, such as "there are

ten thousand school children in this county at the present time and that number increases by twenty-four pupils each day," is about as much as listeners can be expected to remember. If later on in your speech you would like to use a set of figures to establish a point, draw them on a blackboard, or bring them in on large cards. If you begin with a statement, your problem is to make it stick. It's a structural part of your argument. You'll need it around at the finish, so the objective is to make sure your point doesn't dissolve before then.

ANECDOTES

We made a great fuss about anecdotes before. We said you needed them for pace, and that their use marked the difference between the amateur and the pro. Well, they're even more than that. They are also the adhesive that will make your statements and your dry facts and figures stick. In most instances, the fact will not remain long in its complete and total form in the listener's mind—but the story that illustrated it will. The reason is, if you will remember, that these little stories which occur visually in the mind as they are told are easy to remember. You will recall that when we first spoke of the Speech-O-Gram we made quite a point of the fact that it is easy to remember, like the story of the little girl at dancing school who forgot to put on her panties.

Well, just as they are easy for you, the speech-giver, to remember, they are also easy for each member of the audience, the speech-hearer, to remember. When you looked over the Speech-O-Gram you may have been surprised how often it said "Story." Then, when we talked of getting material, emphasis was placed on finding stories or anecdotes to support your statements as you went along. This is where all that begins to pay off.

The Speech-O-Gram, with all its emphasis on pace, has two designs: an inside design and an outside one. First, it is divided into parts, and each part has a job to do at a certain tempo; that is for over-all or outside pace. But then we know there is the pace of the moment itself; that is the pace of what is happening now.

If you pile fact upon fact, you may build up the strongest argument in the world—but everyone will forget what you say as fast as you say it. You've overworked the comprehension rate of the human mind, leaving no time for mental relief by giving them something easy to assimilate between these heavy doses—or, more important, something they can "see" with the mind's eye and remember.

So, you see, the importance of those anecdotes that come before or after each statement grows more and more as we go along. It is impossible to overemphasize their importance. You need them. You can't get along without them.

Your Advance will be in one, two, or three or more parts, just as you listed it in the Objectives section of the Jump-Off. Each part will be made up of statements and facts, the components of the argument you are presenting. Each of these—or as many as possible—should be illustrated by an anecdote.

Let this be your rule: *Don't pour on the heavy fuel too fast or you'll put out the fire.*

It's like the story of the man who . . . well, we won't tell you the rest. We just wanted you to feel that pause of relief and that perking up of interest that comes whenever someone begins talking that way. Why does this happen? Because the speaker is talking your language. You know it's going to be easy to take. It will be a visual mental picture, something to remember.

But try to remember a speech that is made up of a lot of statements strung together like this: "A survey shows that most children between the ages of ten and fourteen have a tendency to . . ." One isn't so bad. But then it becomes one to go with two, and two with four, and up past a few hundred, and it's impossible. Anecdotes are the saving grace for all this, the only difference between boredom and entertainment.

Perhaps you think we harp on anecdotes just a little too much. Well, we can't. It isn't possible. As you begin filling in the Advance, use them as liberally as possible in support of the facts you bring out. There's no such thing as an overdose of anecdotes.

HANDLING HELPS AUDIENCES REMEMBER

A wise man has said, "Clearness ornaments profound thoughts." Keep this maxim foremost in your thinking as you proceed through the Advance.

If you have the slightest doubt that what you say will be understood, your first thought should be, "How can I make it clear?" Simple figures and appropriate stories have already been suggested. Other ways are available; all you need is a little imagination.

The young editor's use of the magazine as a "visual assist" showed excellent handling, drew the eyes away from him and made him feel more comfortable. At the same time, the entire content of his talk unfolded before the eyes as well as the ears of the audience. Without the magazine, his talk would have been complicated and difficult to follow because of the many items he needed to discuss. The "visual" cleared up each point as he went along.

The outline of the box as used in the speech "Meeting the Public at Sidewalk Level," quickly demonstrated a human frailty, or the shortness of the attention span.

Another "help" idea, one which resulted in one of the most talked-about speeches of recent times, was planned and executed by a psychologist, who told his audience about the intensely sickening odor of a liquid he had before him in a corked bottle. He built up the idea in their imagination, then he uncorked the bottle, stood back and watched the reactions. A few people were able to give a very exact description of the smell. Others became so disturbed by the odor that they had to leave the room. In the end, he revealed that the liquid was tap water.

Certainly, this man's "handling help" was effective. His demonstration showed concisely the power of the imagination. Only a few words were required to make his point. The bottle of water had done the rest.

His speaking part consisted mostly in the build-up that preceded the uncorking. Afterward, he asked for listener reactions regarding the smell. Finally, after revealing that the liquid was plain water, he told them that the experiment demonstrated an important characteristic of the imagination.

In choosing a "visual," let simplicity be your ideal. Elaborate displays have a way of cluttering the audience's perspective. Charts, drawings, motion pictures, slides, recordings are fine if they're absolutely necessary to what you're talking about. But, as a rule, who has time to prepare them?

At the Command and General Staff College in Fort Leavenworth, Kansas, many unusual ideas for visual aids were used. One still remembered by many officers in training there was a panorama of the field of battle with all phases of the operation, including bomb blasts, firing, air maneuvers, produced in miniature. This demonstration was used successfully a few times, but after a few mechanical breakdowns and poor timing it was discontinued. It was too complicated.

Officers at the school found that it was wise to keep visual aids simple so as to avoid embarrassing difficulties. Another early discovery was that a "trial run" is necessary, especially when mechanical items are used to help demonstrate the ideas in the speech.

An Army physician found, after an embarrassing experience, the wisdom of checking even the simplest "visual" before he used it. His assigned subject required demonstrating to a small group how upon deep inhalation the air escapes through the nose when the mechanisms of the mouth are not used properly. He used a small mirror which he planned to hold under his nose to demonstrate how it would cloud over when air escaped from the nose at the wrong time. He carried the mirror in his pocket; it was warm there, and when he was ready to demonstrate, it did not cloud. His equipment was simple enough, but his handling failed. All he accomplished was to get a good-natured laugh from his audience when they and he realized that his demonstration was a "bust."

A "handling help"—whether it be some figures, a magazine in the hands of listeners, a simple diagram on a blackboard, or a mechanical item you are demonstrating—should be used only to make the idea stick in the memory of the listeners, never as a kind of side show. Used the latter way, it might make the audience "lose" your speech and recall only the act you put on.

A "visual," if it's simple and entirely to the point, can be effectively used on the Advance. But never force it into the act. If you see the right spot, put it on your bill. It's a good extra added attraction, if its entire effect is to serve the purpose of your speech.

ADVANCE UPHILL

A long time ago, Shakespeare pointed out that "The heavens themselves, the planets and this centre observe degree, priority and place . . . in all line of order." The safe law applies as you line up the two or three principal points in the Advance.

The rule of logical order should be observed so that your audience will be able to follow your speech easily. In addition, you must build the strength of the speech, gradually increasing audience enthusiasm, as you move through the Advance toward the Assault.

Normally, materials in your talk dictate the arrangement. If points contain a time element, then audience thinking follows more easily when they are presented in chronological order, from earliest to latest, or from past to present to future. Speeches on the air power of the United States, the celebration of a national holiday, the work of a humanitarian organization, the growth of a child, the development and use of aluminum or the history of world wars naturally fall into such a category and are most readily handled in sequence of time.

Another prescription for logical arrangement is that of proceeding from the known to the unknown. For example, a speaker is telling his audience about a new type of oil which is "friction proofing." The use of these words might mean nothing to most of the listeners. He would be talking about something strange and get nowhere fast if he assumed they understood, and failed to tie the terms to known experiences.

However, if he asks, "Have you ever noticed how your sewing machine or your car labors on a cold morning—slowly, jerkily?"

and then explains, "That's partly because the mechanical parts are meeting with resistance caused by contact with the surface upon which they move. This is called friction! After a while the rubbing stimulates circulation and the parts begin to move more smoothly, just as a good massage causes the blood to circulate in your blood stream. 'Friction proof' oil cuts this lag in the moving parts in your car, sewing machine or any other mechanical equipment you own, thus saving the wear and tear. . . ."

Now, the speaker is leading from a familiar situation to understanding of the more involved subject he is talking about.

Handling a speech in this manner is like describing the latest design in automobile windshields as "panoramic" rather than to use such technical terminology as multi-dimensional tri-lateral view glass.

Sometimes, a speech is simply topical, a series of topics that can be arranged in almost any manner because there is no particular order. A good example would be a talk on women's wearing apparel for fall, which includes discussion of new hats, dresses and shoes. Another would be on choices of metals: copper, brass or aluminum for some project.

In such talks it is up to you to decide how to arrange the main points, or how to lead from the least to the most interesting material. You should always try to make the Advance build in interest as it approaches the Assault, making it move uphill all the way. You can do this, one way or another, by proper point arrangement, placing that with least force at the beginning; the second, stronger; the third, still stronger.

Some speakers make the mistake of shooting the whole load in the beginning of the Advance, then allowing the rest to go flat and blow away like dry leaves. It must have been this kind of performance that Billy Rose had in mind when a man offered him a startling proposition: "I'll do an act in your show that will be the greatest sensation ever presented. You can advertise it in advance, and get $100 a ticket. Just put $25,000 in the bank for my wife, then I'll then commit suicide in full view of the audience."

"It's a natural!" said Rose. "But just a minute. What will you do for an encore?"

Whether or not this is a true story, it does demonstrate that whatever you do or say—regardless of the impact of your material—you must follow it with something stronger toward the end.

A novice speaker had been told that he needed to get the attention of the audience immediately at the beginning of his talk. He took the advice to heart, and when he reached the speaker's stand raised his hand high above his head and brought it down on the fragile piece of furniture with such force that the stand came apart. He got audience attention, all right. At first, they were stunned; so was the young speaker. He tried to continue, but the embarrassment he felt almost drove the entire talk from his mind.

The plan to remember, then, is that as you build your argument, as you take up each of the objectives listed in the Jump-Off and develop it point by point and illustrate these points with anecdotal references (there we go again!), you are advancing always in one direction—uphill. You are now coming to the Assault, which is the high point in your speech. The only way to get there is by ascension.

CHAPTER **9**

THE
ASSAULT

A<small>T THE CLOSE OF THE JUMP-OFF YOU</small>
made a promise. Ah! There's an old rule
about that. Promises honorably made must
be honorably kept. Your job in the Assault
is to make sure that there is no doubt that
you have fulfilled that promise.

This is the time to stress the advantages,
the truth, the gains in efficiency—whatever
it is that will come through what you have
been talking about. You will recall that the
speaker who spoke on "Meeting the Public
at Sidewalk Level" at this point emphasized how the method he described would
make his listeners' work easier, more enjoyable, more effective! He gave them the
specifics on what this would do for them.

The promise made earlier was answered.

So, think back to your promise. Fulfill it.
Answer it in terms of your audience's bene-
fit, emphasizing what the ideas, plans or
information you have advanced will mean
to them. Hit it hard. Don't hesitate now to
say, "This is your answer," or "This is to

your advantage because. . . ." Be specific, direct, unfaltering. In other words, pull out all the stops. This is the climax of your talk.

If you've said you were going to show them how to solve one of their problems, now is the time to stress the solution. Do it the way the clubwoman did who was talking about the home training program of the United States Army Reserve. In her Advance she told who was eligible, explained the bi-monthly drill formations, the pay for participants, social functions and other features. Then, in the Assault, she summed up the value of such a program to mothers who want to have their sons at home and, at the same time, want to see America prepared and strong.

If you have told your audience they should go to the polls and vote, tell them now how they will profit as individuals by doing so. If it's a how-to speech, even though you have accomplished your purpose of showing them "how" in your Advance, you need to tie the whole thing together in the Assault by pointing up the values of proceeding in the way you have outlined.

This technique is similar to the way a top-flight automobile salesman, for example, goes to some length to make the prospective buyer picture himself driving a beautiful car with all eyes on him, the proud owner. In the Assault you make your listener picture himself enjoying the result of what you offer.

Assume that your speech is on something as everyday as a "how-to" on stamp collecting. A good promise to make would be that you intend to show that spare moments spent in this pursuit can be educational and profitable. Then, after going into the background of stamp collecting in the Advance, you fulfill the promise by showing how they can increase their collections through an exchange program—without cost!

Everyone knows the dangers involved in the failure to keep promises. Anyone who has made that mistake has learned promptly that he'd better keep his next one. Charles Kettering said in one of his speeches, "This is a universe of results or consequences." So, if your talk holds a promise—and what speech worth its salt shouldn't?—you'd better fulfill it. The Assault is the place to make certain that you have.

The main objective of any speech is *that it leads to a useful end for the listener*. Usefulness is always a standard by which you can judge the value of your speech, and it is a promise of usefulness you must make and keep.

The Assault, like other parts of speech, needs the strength that stories, simple statistics and quotations can give it. In fact, it is a good place to use the best and most conclusive you have, because it's the climax of your talk, the highest point of your appeal.

A speaker on the subject "What We Owe Our Children" told in his Assault the story of a little boy who, when darkness came, worried about tigers. To him, they were everywhere. Then one night while the boy was sitting with his father, he slipped his hand beneath his father's arm and said, "When I'm with you Daddy, I'm not afraid of anything. All the tigers run away."

This story summed up the entire idea of the speech. It showed the important part parents play in the lives of their children, not only in protection, but also in companionship, guidance and education. It carried power, illustrating the theme the speaker had been working on throughout—how to keep our children emotionally sound.

A San Antonio businessman, talking to a group of young people, spoke on "America, a Real Land of Promise." He showed that success can and often does come early to men and women in the United States, if they follow certain tenets that are not too difficult to see. Then, as he reached the climax in the Assault, he made the statement that over seven hundred present business leaders achieved the top rung in their companies before reaching the age of thirty-nine—and seventy-five of these were millionaires!

The all-important Assault can make your speech a howling success, or, if omitted, can leave the listeners up in the air saying vaguely to themselves, "Yes, I realize all that, but what does it add up to?"

Really, the Assault is a continuation of the Advance. The same technique of using facts illustrated by anecdotes applies. But it is the high point, the compelling point and—more than anything else—the place where you make certain that the promise you made earlier, both to the audience and yourself, has been kept. It is for this reason more than any other that the Assault is given separate identity in the Speech-O-Gram.

It is the place you prove your promise! Support it with the best arguments and anecdotes you have, the ones that gather up and prove all you have said before. You made a promise earlier, you tell them, and here it is—the proof!

THE MOP-UP

You have finished now and you should tell your audience so. Use a fast clean-up, nail down your main points, throw in a punch line of encouragement to spark future action and enthusiasm. And that's all!

Your job in this phase of your talk is to *tell 'em what you've told 'em*—but fast! You told them once briefly in the Jump-off; you elaborated on this and built your points in the Advance. Now you reiterate this quickly, for the last time. This repetition helps to create the over-all effect of your speech and make the ideas stick in memory—an all-important law of learning.

There are three important *don'ts* to keep in mind when you reach this stage of your speech:

1. *Don't dawdle!*
2. *Don't add forgotten or spur-of-the-moment details!*
3. *Don't overstay your time!*

Commit any of these errors and you detract from the effectiveness of your talk. In fact, you may ruin it.

La Rochefoucauld put it this way: "True eloquence consists in saying all that is necessary, and nothing but what is necessary."

Your opening for this final phase might be worded as follows:

"You have been most courteous in listening to me. I want to be just as courteous and close promptly. However, let me say once again . . . and quickly. . . ."

For the last words, you can throw in a punch line that will encourage actions, enthusiasm, the new way of doing things that you have brought out. Or you might end with a quotation or a light touch of philosophy that wraps up the impression you want to leave with them.

To sum up, these are the *do's* and *don'ts* once again:

• *Use a fast clean-up.*

• *Prepare your audience for the close by saying you are about to do so. This will avoid any embarrassing abruptness.*

• *Nail down your points. Tell 'em what you told 'em. Don't introduce any new details.*

• *Throw in a final punch line of encouragement or saying or remark that has the effect of putting the final stamp on all you've said.*

• *Sit down.*

Write your close in the Mop-up portion of the Speech-O-Gram. Your job is done.

10

OFF
THE
CUFF

PERHAPS YOU THOUGHT WE WOULD FORGET all about the businessman in Chapter 1 who was called on to speak suddenly and unexpectedly, the one who hemmed and hawed and later regretted the important opportunity he'd lost. Perhaps you also thought that the person who can just get up and talk on the spur of the moment is a phenomenon.

Well, we disagree.

"I wish I could think on my feet like that," people say when they have listened to one of these trigger-quick presentations. But once you know the trick, it isn't as phenomenal as it seems.

A young man, well known for his civic leadership in St. Louis, frequently finds himself in the position where he must jump to his feet and give a short speech. He does this so expertly that he has earned a city-wide reputation for superlative spot presentations.

On one occasion he was asked to present diplomas to five hundred high-school graduates. But the program chairman failed to tell him that he would be expected to give a short speech prior to his hand-shaking and sheepskin-passing stint.

During the main speech, the school principal leaned over and suggested, "Better keep your talk to ten minutes." He gulped, and who wouldn't? A sea of five thousand faces, ten thousand ears, would be focused on him three minutes from now and he would have to be good!

He made no excuses. There was no time for that. He just said, "Right!"

As soon as the main address was over, he was introduced. He moved to the speaker's stand as though he'd been waiting for days to have the privilege of talking with these graduates and their parents. His talk afterward brought comments such as, "What you said meant a thousand times more to those kids than that long address by the main speaker." It lasted only nine minutes and forty seconds.

Surprisingly, when the same thing happened to him anywhere else—at a luncheon club, businessmen's convention, lodge meeting—he did as well.

Actually, on these seemingly impromptu occasions, he was giving prepared speeches. He had taken time to jot down notes suitable to five likely situations, sorting out salient points and finding some interesting stories and quotations. Then, he boiled each of them down on 2 x 3-inch cards that fitted into his billfold.

When he suspected he might be called on for a talk, he would review a card and talk it over aloud to himself while waiting for stop lights to change from red to green on his way to the meeting. Once he had presented a talk, he would toss the card away and create a new one.

He was ready at the graduation exercise because, nestled warmly in his hip pocket, was a speech suited to young people. In the three minutes he had before his speech, he took out a card, glanced over it, and put it away. Then he was ready.

He had gone to a little advance trouble, but you can see how it paid off. The value of being able to do something like that is hard to measure generally, but there is no doubt about the impression it leaves. People recognize that anyone who can meet such situations easily is out of the ordinary.

Most people flounder when called upon for an off-the-cuff speech. One of the most common remarks is: "I didn't have the slightest idea I'd be called on." Then there follow a few more excuses and some trite remarks.

That is, usually it happens that way. But why get caught with your vocal equipment down? In this day when anyone can be expected to be called on for "a few words," everyone, except possibly a recluse, should be ready to make a short speech at almost any time.

It's a very good rule when you're headed for a group meeting of any kind to ask yourself one question: "Might I be called on to speak?" Then, if there is the slightest indication you might, be prepared.

The prevailing notion that off-the-cuff speeches are completely unprepared, that they're the output of a certain kind of facile genius, a person born that way, is far from true in most cases. Very few people can jump to their feet under a full head of inspiration and start talking without preparation of one kind or another, and for most it is sheer folly even to try it.

The answer is the same as the Boy Scout motto: "Be Prepared!"

Build these "shorties" around subjects you know about. Familiarity doesn't breed contempt here, but rather, a dash of confidence. Include among your materials ideas you've been discussing with others in ordinary conversation. The more often you've said a thing, the easier it is to talk about it before an audience. The reason that extemporaneous speeches you hear have an air of being spontaneous and casual is because of this, not because the speaker isn't prepared. You've heard comics joke about the rehearsing they had to do for an "ad lib" program. Well, that's the idea.

The short version of the Speech-O-Gram, which you'll meet in just a moment, is planned for these "shorty" speeches. And you can make one up on an ordinary size piece of paper, fold it and place it in your wallet.

Now, if you are in the same position as the young man from St. Louis, you too can have two or three of these ready at all times. You will have one advantage over most impromptu speakers: your short speech will also have form. It is best just before speaking to glance over the short Speech-O-Gram and then put it away before you stand up. Otherwise, you might destroy the illusion that these little speeches are the result of sudden inspiration—which of course they are not.

In brief, this is what you must know: Effective off-the-cuff speaking is simply a matter of preparing for a seemingly unprepared talk. Anticipate that you may be called upon, find a few ideas close to the base of your personal experience, organize them into a plan by using the short Speech-O-Gram. Gradually, by doing this, you will so fix the formula of Jump-off, Advance, Assault and Mop-up into your thinking that you will mentally organize such speeches without the need of notes.

On the next page is your short Speech-O-Gram.

Speech-O-Gram
(for short talks)
JUMP-OFF:

<u>Objective A:</u> (Establish kinship) _____

_____
_____
_____
_____

<u>Story:</u> _____

_____
_____
_____
_____

ADVANCE: (Point out that...) _____

_____
_____

(Story) _____

_____

ASSAULT: (Bear down) _____

_____
_____

MOP-UP: (Tighten the vise) _____

_____

CHAPTER **11**

FOR
SPEAKING
OUT LOUD

YOU HAVE COMPLETED YOUR SPEECH-O-Gram and there's still some time before you give your speech. What do you do now?

You've been told there's nothing to worry about, that the speech is all there, in a form you can't forget. The idea is to prove this to yourself. Read it over two or three times and then take a forgetting test. Put the speech away, then think about one, or several, or all of the following fourteen things:

1. What did I have for breakfast this morning?
2. What appointments do I have coming up during the next seven days?
3. What is each member of my family doing at the present moment?
4. What letters do I need to write?
5. What repairs does my car need just now?
6. How far do I travel each day in my work?

77

7. How can I make my work more effective?

8. How much will my income tax amount to this year?

9. How can I make more money than I am earning at present?

10. Approximately what is my net worth?

11. What jobs need to be done around the house?

12. Am I caught up on my "thank you" letters?

13. Who is the Secretary of State?

14. When is the next General Election?

Now speak your speech aloud. Call this your rehearsal. See if you've left anything out. The chances are that it is fixed in your mind and you can be assured you are prepared.

Now, if you have enough time, go over the speech a few times, using various ways and phrases to express the ideas. Get your tongue accustomed to saying the words; tell the stories, repeat the maxims and the statistical facts a few times. This will help to make the words fall easily into place when you stand before your audience, and you will gain greater confidence.

One speaker we know believes so strongly in the value of this phase of preparation that he follows the rule of giving his talk aloud eight times within the twenty-four-hour period prior to delivery; three of these oral rehearsals he schedules for the last two hours before speech time. This is good practice and certainly adds to his assurance that the speech is fixed in his brain and on his tongue.

But with the Speech-O-Gram, this extra effort really isn't necessary. The continual use of the Speech-O-Gram format eliminates the time-consuming practice of lengthy revision. Just discussing the content of the speech with others and saying it aloud two or three times is all that is really necessary to lodge it safely for future delivery. The days of oratory when speeches were memorized or read are past. So let your preparation make it so—know it, but don't read or memorize it. You'll kill the entire effect.

Summing it up: once you've finished the Speech-O-Gram, let your talk stand as is. Read it over two or three times aloud. Put it aside and let your mind ramble through a detour such as the one given. Then try the speech aloud.

If time is available, talk with friends about the content of your talk and run over the speech aloud two or three more times to fix it in your speech mechanisms.

Now you're all set. Just relax. And we'll get to that in the next chapter.

CHAPTER **12**

AT EASE
ON THE
PLATFORM

A NATIONALLY KNOWN LECTURER WAS telling us recently about his early experiences with speech-making and how he learned to control his excitement in speaking situations.

"I made a very important discovery during my early teens," he recalled, "which has helped in every speech I have given since. I was to speak at a church service along with three other young people and my speech was to be last. As the time drew near for me to step up to the pulpit, I noticed that I was becoming tense, that my breathing rate was beginning gradually to speed up. I knew that if I didn't do something about it, I would be in no condition to give my talk. There was still time, so I decided to try to slow it down. I started to count silently at a slow rate, one . . . two . . . three . . . four . . . and so on, taking a breath between each number. The

81

technique worked excellently for me, and when I was called on I was more relaxed and my breathing was regular again. I use the same device today when I'm faced with a challenging subject or audience, and it always helps."

It is obvious, of course, that this speaker was working on the mind and body at once. He was using the mind to run off the exercise, thereby not giving it a chance to fill up with imaginary fears, and he was controlling the body by methodical ventilation. On his own, he had discovered a vital key in self-control, one which is important in public speaking for a number of reasons.

Smooth, easy, regular breathing and a calm state of brain and body go together. One complements the other. You know what happens to your breathing when you are excited. It comes in short, fast gasps which are usually irregular. On the other hand, when you are calm and peaceful it is slow and even. Since you need to be as relaxed as possible during a presentation, a controlled breathing pattern should be used to obtain it.

And, too, the air you inhale becomes the raw material for voice—the water which makes the mill wheel go 'round in vocalization. The outflowing air stream causes your vocal cords to vibrate, thus producing the sounds you make as you speak. Unless the air flows evenly and smoothly, your voice will sound breathy and your speaking may become jerky.

In this age of microphones, obvious breathing is picked up and broadcast to the listeners. Unless it is controlled, your audience may listen to your stentorian intakes of air rather than to your ideas. Consciously or unconsciously, you too will realize that all is not well and your irregular and noisy breathing will add to your excitement and tension.

As you sit waiting for your turn to speak, you need to keep your breathing as nearly normal as possible. If the rate tends to increase despite your best intentions, there are three methods which have been tested and found satisfactory by speakers. Each is a variation of the other and your choice is only a matter of which suits you best.

1. Think to yourself that you should breathe regularly; command yourself to inhale slowly ... pause ... exhale slowly.
2. Use the lecturer's device: count one, then inhale slowly, pause, exhale slowly; count two, inhale slowly, pause, exhale slowly; and so on.
3. If neither of these devices work effectively, try counting: one, two, three, four, five, inhale slowly; one, two, three, four, five, exhale slowly; and so on.

Surely one of these will ease your tensions some. But if a quiver of excitement remains, a certain edginess, don't let it worry you. There are those who maintain you must feel some of this to be "right." And, anyway, we'll guarantee a small miracle will take place when you start talking, when you get a few sentences into this speech which you know is well prepared. You'll forget completely there ever was such a thing as nervousness.

PLATFORM "UNLAXATION"

Relaxation—what is it? One New Yorker was asked that question and he replied, "Oh, that's what happens when you are dead."

We do not want to get into the subject of general relaxation because that is a book in itself. What we are concerned with is temporary relaxation, so that the waiting period before a speech won't tie your "innards" into a knot.

A Richmond, Virginia, businessman was one of many in this high-powered age who was faced with this problem. Although he planned good speeches and did a fair job with them on the platform, his nervousness and consequent bizarre movements detracted from what he had to say. The audience watched him pull at his nose, scratch his chest, and pace back and forth on the platform. He recognized his problem, but each new speaking experience found him repeating the same errors.

Finally, he came to us for help. He was asked to sit down for a short time and relax. When we checked him after five minutes, we found that his body was as stiff as a bedpost. He was unable to relax.

After five sessions and careful coaching, he learned to free himself from the tension and his presentations improved. The exercises we used with him are the same as those used in speech clinics where people who tend toward extreme tenseness in the time preceding a speech come for help. For them (and for you, if you have the problem) it's best to start these exercises several days before a speaking assignment.

Here goes:

Stand erect. Slowly raise the arms out to the sides, up to shoulder level, inhaling as you do. Clench the fists and tense the muscles of the arms. Hold for five seconds. Then, suddenly, let the breath go; relax the arms and hands. Don't push them down, but let them fall. Repeat several times. This exercise makes you feel the difference between ordinary muscle tonus and tension in your arms. When you can do this correctly, it teaches you that you can instantly free the muscles from tension at your own mental command. And it is in your muscles, don't forget, that tension resides.

Now, twist the upper trunk, one shoulder forward and then the other, using a "shimmy" movement in slow motion, allowing the arms to flop loosely and keep the freedom in the arms that you felt after you dropped them to your sides in the previous exercise.

Next, stand erect and raise the arms slowly from the sides up over the head, stretching them toward the ceiling and going up on the toes, inhaling once throughout the movement. Hold tensely while you count to three. Now, let your entire body relax, and fall into a squatting position, exhaling as you go. Rest there for a few moments and then rise slowly to erect position. Repeat several times, until you really let yourself go as you fall. Now you are freeing the muscles of the legs, trunk and arms so that the entire body falls for lack of muscle tension.

Stretch out on a cot, think about the various parts of the body, starting with the feet and going up—legs, hips, back, chest, neck, face, relaxing or "letting go" each part. Then, think quieting thoughts while someone tests your arms and legs by moving them about easily to make certain that they are free from tension. Have your helper roll your head from side to side and move the jaw down and up to determine whether these parts are relaxed.

The first three exercises serve to show you the difference between tension and relaxation in the body's parts; the last helps to maintain the relaxed bodily state for a period of time. Take a few minutes each day for these exercises.

We have found, after working with thousands of individuals over the past twenty years, that anyone can improve his ability to relax voluntarily. And so can you.

Now let's take one more step—up onto the speaker's platform.

The best place to fasten your attention is not on yourself, but on what others are doing and saying. (Remember the pleasant thoughts on the couch?) As you wait to be introduced, keep your breathing from running away with itself, as suggested in the preceding chapter.

But, you say as you sit there, it's easier said than done. There's a spot near your eye that feels as though it might start twitching despite everything. This is still all right. You are not striving for such tranquility and peace of mind that you might nod off to sleep; you want just a reasonable degree of control. You look at the veteran speaker two chairs away, observe how quietly he sits, and think he's not bothered by anything like this. Well, not for a moment! He's got that "platform feeling" too. The only difference between you and him is that he knows these things are to be expected, and that once things get going they have a way of taking care of themselves.

AUDIENCES ARE NICE PEOPLE

There's a secret that every speaker knows which you might as well be in on from the start. Actually, and with very few exceptions, audiences are made up of nice people who want you to do well. They're like the general who while inspecting troops would check a man's gear, then salute and say, "Me, too!"

After several salutes and "Me, too's!" his aide ventured, "If you'll pardon the impertinence, sir, I would like to ask why you salute these privates and say, 'Me, too!' " The general paused in his inspection and explained, "You see, I came up through the ranks myself and I know just what they're thinking. So, I tell 'em, 'Me, too!'"

Many of your listeners have been through the experience of giving a speech and they are able to say "Me, too!" They know how you feel about the entire task and they're in there pitching with you.

A college president had gone to great trouble to speak to a group in Detroit and his ideas stimulated considerable question-asking afterwards. His answers were direct and quick, until one questioner slowed him with a specific question requiring some research he had not made. He could have bluffed it, but instead he said, "I can't give you the answer right off, but if you'll give me your name and address, I'll send it to you by return mail." When the speech was over the listener apologized for putting the speaker on the spot. He said that he really wanted to know the answer but rather than cause the speaker trouble, he would do some research himself.

Most listeners are like that. They don't want to embarrass the speaker or cause him any trouble. You need to recognize this quality in your audience and make an early attempt to set yourself at ease regarding their attitudes. The best time to do this is before you go to the speaker's stand. Get there early and circulate among those who will be listening later. Look for people you know, shake hands, talk with them. It is good to realize you have friends out there. Have your host or hostess or the chairman introduce you around. A friend of ours makes this a regular practice and reports, "The introductions to members of my audience help to break the ice for me, easing my start when I get to the platform. It seems, really, that all I have to do when I'm called on to speak is continue my conversation with them, and this of course works wonders in eliminating the strangeness of the situation and decreasing emotional tensions."

Your "casing" job can get you started on this. When you learned the interests of these people you learned a lot about them. Maybe you even met a few. So now let your conversation be concerned with their problem just as your speech will be later.

And there's this to remember about audiences too: they're really easier on you than you are on yourself, and are not so sensitive to your little bobbles. Should you make a "goof" as you talk, don't worry about it too much. Just go ahead. Par for the course allows for a few of these.

Use the following practical suggestions for easing those moments before you speak:

1. Get there early, circulate, talk with those you meet or know in the audience.
2. Ask someone in charge to introduce you about. Handshakes, smiles, conversations all help.
3. Then, when you get up on the platform, remember that audiences are nice people.

CHAPTER **13**

START
FROM A
STOP

Leonardo da Vinci was known to be a very deliberate painter, sometimes staring at his canvas for long periods of time before making a stroke with his brush. One day he explained those long waits to his friends: "When I pause longest," he told them, "I make the most telling strokes with my brush."

In public speaking also the pauses are important. And when you make them you make your "most telling strokes" with words.

Recently, at a political rally, we observed how neatly a major campaigner got under way with his presentation. Seated in the audience, the popular candidate came to the podium in the midst of enthusiastic applause. He walked smilingly through the audience, shaking hands with friends and waving to those out of reach. The cheering continued after he reached the platform.

He shook hands with the dignitaries, then moved to the speaker's stand, arranged his notes, waited silently. Gradually, the noise subsided and he began to speak.

This speaker realized the importance of starting from a stop. Had he begun his talk sooner, the audience would have missed his opening. As it was, he made efficient use of the "magic moment of silence" between arrival at the stand and the time he started to speak.

During this period, many favorable things happened to ease his presentation and make him appear a more effective speaker. His silence was a wand waved over the heads of his audience, making them quiet, drawing them together into a listening, thinking group, no longer a disorganized mob.

Audiences need time for these things. If you start talking too soon, they take time to settle down anyway, and miss what you are saying. Naturally, you do not want to make this pause too long or it may seem that you are at a loss for words. In most instances, it should last only a few seconds because audiences are usually quiet and waiting for you to speak once you have been introduced.

This starting from a stop is recommended over any other approach because it indicates poise and control on your part and has a relaxing effect on the audience. This is the best procedure:
1. Stand before your audience, thereby giving them time to look you over.
2. Then place your notes.
3. Look over your audience again as you consider your first words.
4. Start speaking.

Your mannerisms from this point on will have a lot to do with the effectiveness of your presentation. And knowing these, getting a mirror's view of yourself, is especially important if you intend to speak often in public. At least you should avoid some of the major errors.

J. M. O'Neill, one of the great teachers of public speaking, once said, "Practice makes permanent, not perfect." He meant that if you continue to repeat your errors they become fixed habit patterns.

The frequent bad mannerisms that harm a speech come in six common garden varieties:

1. *Sagging and Dragging.* This includes poor posture, hanging the head, slumping on the speaker's stand, and scraping the soles and heels on the way to the podium.
2. *Dressing and Messing.* The speaker nervously brushes the air, picks imaginary lint off the jacket, straightens the tie, winds his watch, drums with the fingers, fumbles with keys, pulls at girdle, and so on.
3. *Never-moving or Overdoing.* The speaker has a tendency to get stuck in one place and remain there, position-glued, throughout the speech; or, he wanders aimlessly and without purpose in a kind of St. Vitus dance around the podium.
4. *Dead-pan.* This is a failure to allow the face to convey feelings behind words; the expression is set, never changing with the ideas the speaker wants to get across.
5. *Faraway Look.* The speaker's eyes study everything in the room except the audience—the walls, floor, ceiling, his notes—and he has no idea what kind of reaction he is getting from his hearers.
6. *Unheard Voice.* The words are either muffled and indistinct, or the voice is weak, thin or "talked down." The audience must strain to hear what the speaker is saying.

The opposites of these unpleasant habits are, of course, what you should strive for on the platform: good posture, with the crown of the head held high; an I-mean-business walk; purposeful body movements used sparingly; responsive facial expression; direct eye contact; an adequate voice that brings clarity to the words it speaks.

Hard to do? No! You have prepared a speech worth hearing and that means you're worth listening to.

CHAPTER 14

SUMMING
IT
UP

To IMPROVE THE GOLDEN MOMENT OF opportunity, and catch the good that is in our reach, is the great art of life." So said Samuel Johnson.

An invitation to speak may be an "opportunity"; in fact, it may well be your "golden moment of opportunity." You never know who is out there listening, taking your measurements for a more important, better-paying job.

The story goes that a certain Midwestern university had invited a man to come halfway across the United States to present a talk at a convocation. He felt that if they thought that much of him and his abilities as a speaker, he should do his best. Little did he realize that the real purpose was to size him up for the presidency of the institution. His speech was one of the tests the board of trustees used as a measuring rod of a candidate's mental stature and ability.

Fortunately for him, he turned out a top-flight speech. He got the job.

This story isn't so unusual. We could cite a good many more instances to go with it. But the point we would rather make is that the ability to speak well works two ways. You gain prestige in the eyes of others and (perhaps more important) confidence in yourself. Gradually you untie the imaginary ropes that may have slowed your rise to success in your particular field. Having read this book, you have solid ground on which to walk, so go ahead confidently. A chance to speak now can be a bright spot instead of a dread one on your horizon—because you know how!

The Speech-O-Gram, as we said before, isn't as important as the wheel was to civilization. But it is the reason you can be sure. It has been thoroughly tested under control conditions and has been proved to work!

Now, briefly and quickly, let's run through the process by which the Speech-O-Gram operates. Then you're on your own.

Once you accept an invitation to speak, your first thought of course is, "What shall I talk about?" Interest factors will determine your choice. You should choose a subject suited to the interests of your audience, and one that you are enthusiastic about. Your listeners should be your first consideration. The choice will depend upon their age, sex, occupations, problems, enthusiasms, objectives. In other words, "case" your audience.

If possible, choose a current subject and one that you know something about. Your interest in your topic will make it a part of you; as a result, your confidence and your effectiveness will improve.

Once the topic is decided upon, the next step is mobilization. Put your own thoughts on paper and gather additional material on a shopping tour at the public library. As you do, keep a sharp lookout for illustrations that will back up the points you wish to make—anecdotes, experiences, maxims, quotations, statistical proof. These are the "life" of your speech.

Now use the Speech-O-Gram to mold the materials into a forward-moving speech. Each phase of the Speech-O-Gram (Scoop,

Jump-off, Advance, Assault, Mop-up) has a definite and inter-related purpose. As you put your speech together, refer again to those chapters which deal with these phases. Just a fast, hoppity-skip reading should be enough.

Once the Speech-O-Gram is filled in, run the speech over to yourself once or twice. Such a "shake-down" will tell you quickly if there's anything of which you're not as sure as you'd like to be. Perhaps you may want to make a few changes. For that reason it is best to use a pencil.

You now have the perfect requisite for confidence: a well-organized speech with a high-level interest content. You've got it made, so get out of the strait jacket of concern and relax. Size up your audience for what they are—just folk, like yourself, who are going to be with you every inch of the way. They're nice people!

Control your breathing. One ... inhale; two ... exhale. But don't let a few ripples of excitement in your stomach bother you. Every speaker feels this, and you can be certain they'll disappear once you begin to talk.

Make it a rule to pause a moment before you start. This "starting from a stop" is the only way to open a speech.

As you talk, use only those movements that help put your ideas across to your listeners. Avoid wasted, nervous moving around. It gives the impression that you lack both poise and confidence.

Stay with the organization you've set for yourself in the Speech-O-Gram. On-the-spot changes may make you wander from the subject and the coming back may be difficult.

As you talk you may learn a new concept of time. It seems to go by in a flash. Speakers often report that ten minutes seemed like one or twenty like two. You've said all you intended and planned and yet, before you know it, your speech is over.

Once you have discovered these techniques and accustomed yourself to using them, you will untie the imaginary knots that kept you on the listener's bench so long. And you will enjoy the experience of presenting your thoughts in public. It's quite a feeling.

II THE SPEECH-O-GRAM

"THE MIND CAN ASSIMILATE ONLY WHAT THE SEAT WILL ENDURE"

Here are 25 sample Speech-O-Grams for a variety of speaking occasions. Just pick one close enough to the speech you must give and, with a little doctoring, it will fit. Or you may want to start all the way from scratch, to find out just how good you can get. Go ahead!

We have given examples of openings for the various parts of the speech, but not the more detailed information you will want to insert. Usually a few words will do this, to remind you that you wish to mention this and that. Put them down after the opening remarks (which are really the transitions of the speech) in each section.

Remember, the Speech-O-Gram is put together in a way to allow for a slip-up. Forget a point or two and you'll still get the job done well.

Speech-O-Gram 1

APPEAL

Sidewalks of New Carlisle

Frequently, people with little experience in public speaking are called upon to present an appeal to a public body, and they lack confidence in their ability to do so. A carefully planned and rehearsed talk will be helpful to individuals faced with this challenge. This type of speech should include: recognition of the body as an important governing group, complimentary remarks regarding its contribution to the community, a clear statement regarding the problem, and—if one is known—a suggested solution. Some humor early in the talk and later will help to ease the situation both for the speaker and the governing body. Such talks should be brief and to the point because, in most instances, these boards usually have on the agenda many items requiring attention at the meeting.

Speech-O-Gram 1: APPEAL

group:_____

address:_____time:_____

title: SIDEWALKS OF NEW CARLISLE

Time
(min.)

SCOOP: Mr. President, ladies and gentlemen
of the city council. I have been observing
you at work and realize that your task is
not an easy one. And I'm afraid my subject
(see title) will by no means simplify it.
I'm here in the strange role of a taxpayer
who wants you to spend money.

JUMP-OFF: My request bears close resemblance
to a definition of thrift I heard once:
Objective A: This has been the attitude in
our community for some time and civic
betterment has failed to keep step with population growth and industrial development.
We have some catching up to do.
Objective B: Therefore, let's look at one
way to start on an improvement program.
Objective C: The considerations will be:
the need for sidewalks in New Carlisle, and
ways and means of obtaining them.
Promise: Perhaps, my few words here today
will start some constructive action which
will relieve a bad situation.

100

ADVANCE: (point 1) First, let's consider
the need.

Story: Saving the taxpayer's money is a good
habit but sometimes it is carried too far.
It's like the time a lady patient at City
Hospital required three blood transfusions.
A brawny Scotsman offered his blood. The
patient gave him $50 for the first pint, $25
for the second pint — but the third time she
had so much Scotch blood in her she only
thanked him.

Our town has been without sidewalks
ever since Cal Jones' grocery was the only
building at the Route 12 intersection.

As we grew, Main and Second were paved
for three blocks. Now, when it rains, the
citizens who walk to town go in to their
ankles and the dry dust in summer makes
everyone look as though he's wearing tan
bobby socks.

ADVANCE: (point 2) Certainly there are
ways and means of overcoming this situation.
Let us consider them for a moment.

Money for the paving can come from two
sources. The county can pay for paving
around the three elementary schools and the
high schools. This will ease the burden on
the city. A levy of one mill in the next
city election, if passed, would provide adequate funds to do the rest of the job.

ASSAULT: Someone has suggested various
piecemeal plans for getting sidewalks in.
Personally, I'm opposed to this — the job
could drag on for years. New Carlisle has
needed these improvements too long. Unless
we keep up in civic betterment with the
sound population and industrial growth we

have experienced in the past, people and industry will go elsewhere. Our city is prospering. Let's keep it that way.

MOP-UP: I know you have much to do in your meeting tonight so I will close by saying that we all appreciate the excellent work the council is doing for our city, and repeat again that the need for sidewalks is great. Means are available for putting them in, and the taxpayers are ready and willing to have it done. Please take steps now to get the entire job done without delay.

Speech-O-Gram 2

ACCEPTANCE

Thank You

Sincerity and depth of appreciation are characteristics of the acceptance speech. The emotional aspects should not be carried too far, however. The occasion is a joyful one and the response by the recipient should be lightened by at least a few touches of humor. The speaker needs to say "thank you" and to express his indebtedness to the group. Although he may be tempted to do so, he should not say too much. A short talk of ten to fifteen minutes is quite adequate for the purposes he needs to accomplish.

Speech-O-Gram 2: ACCEPTANCE

group:_____

address:_____time:_____

title: THANK YOU

Time (min.)	SCOOP: Mrs. Johnson — your chairman — told me that the committee had difficulty choosing this wonderful gift. I'm certain they had no greater problem than my tongue is having as it stumbles to find the words I want for saying (see title).

JUMP-OFF: This occasion calls to mind little Billy's attitude toward the new baby at his house, etc.

Objective A: My fifteen years at Minnesota Mills have been an experience that I will remember always — the pleasant assignment and the friendly people have caused time to flick by like frames on a movie film.

Objective B: Let me take a moment to tell what that time has meant to me.

Objective C: First, I want to say "thank you," wholeheartedly; and second, to express my debt of gratitude to you, my friends and associates.

Promise: My words will allow me to unload my loss in leaving and, perhaps you may come to appreciate your good fortune in staying.

ADVANCE: (point 1) First, I want to say
"thank you."
Story: A gift like this says so much. It is
a token of abiding friendship and love,
quite different from the sentiment expressed
by the young lady who said to her boy
friend, "Did anyone ever tell you how wonderful you are?"

"No," he replied, "I don't believe
anyone ever did."

"Oh," she said, "then I'd wish you'd
tell me where you got the idea."

Seriously, though, I am deeply and
sincerely grateful for your thoughtful gift,
for your many congratulatory letters and
telegrams, and for being here on this delightful and memorable occasion.

ADVANCE: (point 2) My debt to you is
great, not only for these present expres-
sions of kindness, but for what all of you
have done to help make Minnesota Mills one
of the great Taconite producers of the
nation.

When I glance at this beautiful watch,
I will be reminded of your promptness in
keeping appointments, your planning for max-
imum accomplishment in your daily work as-
signments, your good use of each measured
minute at the plant, and for the pleasant
manner in which you worked for improvement
at Minnesota Mills.

ASSAULT: This watch will remind me of all
these contributions on your part, and even
more it will remind me of the thousands of
pleasant hours I spent with this organization.

As John Quincy Adams put it in <u>The Hour Glass</u>:

> "Alas! How swift the moments fly,
> How flash the years along!
> Scarce here, yet gone already by,
> The burden of a song."

MOP-UP: A football player at Indiana University was awarded a large silver cup with his name engraved on it. Upon receiving the gift, he picked up the trophy and said simply, "Shore is pretty." Then he sat down. Again, I'll say your gift "shore is pretty." Thank you for your many kindnesses, your cooperation and the high tribute you have paid me today.

Speech-O-Gram 3

SPEECH TO TEACH

Stuttering

The didactic or informative presentation should be amply illus-trated with examples which clarify the thoughts expressed. In the speech on stuttering, specific cases served this purpose. In other speeches to teach, statistical facts, anecdotes, comparisons and quotations might better suit the material.

The speaker's principal effort in the speech to teach should be to put across the ideas so that they are easily grasped by the audience. The complexity of the presentation will depend upon the level of academic attainment of most of the audience. The successful speaker tries to find out what this is before he makes his preparation for the talk. Then he slants his material accord-ingly.

Speech-O-Gram 3: SPEECH TO TEACH

group:_____

address:_____time:_____

title: STUTTERING

Time
(min.)

○

SCOOP: Mrs. Justice — your chairman — has advised me that all of you are interested in speech problems, in one way or another. For that reason, I decided to talk on (see title),a speciality of mine since entering the field of speech pathology in 1937.

JUMP-OFF: This subject and the occasion call to mind the experiences of John M., a stutterer.

Objective A: Ignorance on the part of others toward this young man proves that there is much more to stuttering than muscle blocking. People need to understand better the psychological aspects and that corrective work is for qualified specialists.

Objective B: Therefore, let us all try to better understand the problem and the people who are so handicapped.

Objective C: First, let us consider the problem in adults and then look to childhood influences that tend to bring on the difficulty.

Promise: Such a discussion should lead to

a better understanding of a problem that
has always been cloaked with mystery.

ADVANCE: (point 1) First, consider the
difficulty as it exists in adults — its
causes, attitudes of those who stutter,
and effects upon personality.
Story: (Tell about stutterer who was waylaid
by the drunk.)
        Various ideas exist as to causes:
handedness, shock, imitation, inheritance,
feeling of inferiority, elongated tongue,
etc.
        Stutterers are barraged with crackpot
ideas, speech crutches and inane suggestions. Result: confusion, embarrassment.
        Early charlatans advertised, "Stut-
tering cured; results guaranteed." Later,
the American Speech and Hearing Association
established a code of ethics and put the
quacks out of business.
        Stuttering is characterized by false
starts, repetitions, blockings, irregular
breathing, avoidance of difficult words
and the use of starters.
        As a whole, stutterers are overly
ambitious and conscientious. They have
common characteristics, but each case requires individual treatment.

ADVANCE: (point 2) Next, let us consider
the problem in young children:
        The case of Jerry B. who responded to
therapy once conditions were corrected at
home.
        Stuttering often begins between the
fifth and eighth years — the "tender years"
when the child leaves the home for the
broader social environment of school.

Numerous factors bring on stuttering: illness, shock, fright, injury, reprimand.

Richard S., seven, started to stutter when appendicitis struck; Calvin S., six, after a near-drowning episode; Harry H., after a narrow escape from falling plaster in an old school building.

ASSAULT: Can the problem be avoided; if so, how?

Teachers and parents can guard against shock, illness and social penalties during the "tender years."

Some children need to have their ego built up — they must be made to realize that they are more adequate than they imagine and that people care for them. They need to learn to relax and, in many instances, slow to a normal pace. Speech fluency is bred of confidence, security and health in a happy home.

MOP-UP: Thus we see stuttering as false starts, hesitations, repetitions, blockings, facial grimaces, tics. It is a complex problem understood by only a few. Many theories prevail as to its cause, but "the cause" has never been discovered. Frequently it starts between the ages five to eight and results from shock to the nervous system. Care and good judgment on the part of adults and playmates can do much toward preventing onset.

Speech-O-Gram 4

SERMON

The Sense of Smile

Sermons, in these modern days, are frequently centered about practical, day-to-day subjects, with the Bible serving as the basic reference for supporting proof. In addition to quotations from the Holy Bible, personal experiences, serious and humorous anecdotes, comparisons and interesting facts are used to develop the theme. The body of the sermon can be outlined effectively in the two-point Advance of the Speech-O-Gram, the first point to include materials relevant to the present-day situation with the second point stressing religious emphases.

Speech-O-Gram 4: SERMON

group:_____

address:_____time:_____

title: THE SENSE OF SMILE

time
(min.)

SCOOP: With very little effort, you could sit down and list one hundred reasons to frown. On the other hand, you could do the same with reasons to smile and be joyful. That's why I will talk today on (see title). You see, I am a Christian, and believe there is reason for great joy in the world today.

JUMP-OFF: The Reverend Doctor Edgar DeWitt Jones propounded the specifications of a good minister: etc.

<u>Objective A:</u> Yes, we should enjoy our religion, the wonderful world about us, the very fact that we are free Americans, living in our beautiful country, God's country if you will, and enjoying many, many blessings.

<u>Objective B:</u> Let us look for these brighter perspectives in our own lives and in the Bible.

<u>Objective C:</u> The important considerations will be: Our attitudes today, and joy in Christian living as exemplified in His Holy Word.

<u>Promise:</u> Having thus approached the sub-

112

ject, you may receive renewed confidence in
your life and gain more from the wonderful
joy of living the Christian life.

ADVANCE: (point 1) First, let us consider
the attitudes of people today, and reasons
why they do not find joy in life.
Story: Recently, I noticed that a young
lady in the congregation was quite glum. I
asked her why, "With conditions as they
are, I wonder if it's worth the effort —
missiles, rockets, atom bombs."
     "There have always been great dangers
— real and imagined — in the world," I
said. "Enjoy life. Love each golden minute
of it."
     That girl was fearful. She was not
living confidently in Christian faith.
     For the "joy that was set before him,
Jesus endured the cross" (Hebrews 12:2).
Knowing this, how can Christians miss the
great joy that comes from living?
     Next time you walk downtown, count
the number of people who have a smile on
their faces. You'll find very few. It
takes more effort to frown than to smile
and there are so many reasons to smile:
God's great gift of friends, good health,
the peace we have, the beauty of nature all
about us, to name a few.

ADVANCE: (point 2) As our next consideration, let us look to the Bible. Does it
suggest that we refrain from joy of living?
     When Jesus' disciples found themselves
successful in furthering His Kingdom they
"were filled with great joy" (Acts 13:52,
15:3). To Paul, the Kingdom was joy, as
well as righteousness and peace (Romans
14:17).

Christianity is the most joyful of
world religions. The Wise Men rejoiced to
find the star that led them to Bethlehem
(Matthew 2:10). Angels announced their
"good tidings of great joy" which was to
"all people" (Luke 2:10). Jesus came into
the world that His joy might be established
in men and made complete (John 15:11).

ASSAULT: Christians in America, and
throughout the world, who live up to the
tenets of their religion have reason for
great joy. Their faith gives them the inner
confidence which casts out doubt and fear.
It causes them to forget "self" and to
think of others. When this happens, a new
sense comes into being — the sense of
smile.

MOP-UP: As I close, let me repeat that
Jesus came into the world that His joy
might be established in men and made complete. As good Christians, all of us should
reflect that joy in our everyday life, look
for it in His Holy Word and develop the
faith that makes our whole life resplendent
in His joy.

Speech-O-Gram 5

ANNOUNCEMENT OF PUBLIC EVENT

Open House at the New Public Library

Announcement speeches should accomplish the following objectives: getting and holding the attention, stating benefits, and giving all of the facts. Humor is used at the beginning and during the statement about *Open House at the New Library* to effect the first purpose. Benefits are brought out under the first point of advance and the specific details are presented in the second point of advance. In announcements such as this one, the speaker must not only inform, he must urge and even inspire. The speech is usually brief but the essential facts should be stated twice: once in the advance and once in the Mop-up.

Speech-O-Gram 5: ANNOUNCEMENT OF PUBLIC EVENT

group:_____

address:_____time:_____

title: OPEN HOUSE AT THE NEW PUBLIC LIBRARY

time
(min.)

SCOOP: Buck — our president — and I were just talking about an important occasion that is close at hand. He felt you would be interested and asked me to make an announcement regarding: (see title). Every civic-minded citizen will be there, as I know you will.

JUMP-OFF: Robert Frost said recently that he has a fine collection of books, and reads them, cover by cover.
Objective A: Mr. Frost's quip expresses the attitude many people have regarding books. We're listening to TV so much that we miss one of the greatest sources of information and understanding.
Objective B: If I can get you over to this Open House, maybe I can start a trend. That's exactly what I want to do.
Objective C: I'll tell you about the bene-fits of attending the Open House and then give you the details as to date, time and place.
Promise: If my announcement accomplishes

116

its purpose, I know you will have a pleasant visit and make interesting discoveries
about books.

ADVANCE: (point 1) What benefits can
accrue to you if you attend this affair?
Story: A man and woman were talking about
their trips to Asia. Neither had been outside the U.S. "The pagodas — did you see
them?" he asked. "See them? I had dinner
with them," she replied.

There are pagodas in the form of
books at the library, but few get that well
acquainted with them.

I know that some of you spend time
with books, but many will be amazed at the
treasury of information available.

You will have a chance to examine
volumes just off the presses on subjects
ranging from jets, rockets and the astronauts, to successful parties, Ty Cobb and
garden shrubs. The classics will be there,
too — and for many, the children and youth
section will be of interest. You will see
several interesting book displays. Refresh-
ments will be served and there will be
special music.

ADVANCE: (point 2) Now for the details as
to time and place.

The Open House will be held Sunday,
December 17, from 2:00 to 4:30, in the
bright and shiny new library on Forrest
Avenue at Mulberry Street, opposite the
old Post Office. You are invited to come
and bring the entire family. It's all free.
Mr. Ronald McFarland, the librarian, will
be on hand to show you around.

ASSAULT: You'll enjoy your visit to the new library. Your hour or so at the Open House will be enlightening and most enjoyable.

The salesman told the big businessman, "I've been trying to see you for a week; may I have an appointment?"

The executive replied, "Make a date with my secretary."

The salesman said, "I did and we had a blast, but I still want to see you."

MOP-UP: I'd suggest that you make a date with your entire family for Sunday, December 17th, 2:00 to 4:30, and get over to the new library at Forrest and Mulberry. You'll enjoy it. So will they!

Speech-O-Gram 6

INTRODUCTION (INFORMAL)

Dr. J. Bruce Wilson

Introductions vary in formality with the situation in which they are presented. This talk—suitable for a civic club or Junior Chamber luncheon—is meant to create a friendly, pleasant relationship between the main speaker and the audience. The person who does the introducing has the important job of paving the way for the speaker, making him feel comfortable and giving him a good send-off.

Usually about all the after-dinner speaker gets for his trouble is a few kind words, and certainly he should receive some favorable comments. A telephone call or two and a little advance research will help the "introducer" find facts about the speaker's educational background and career. The presentation of this information will give satisfaction to the speaker and—like the biographical sketch of an author on the cover packet of a book—give the listener vital clues for understanding the speech.

Speech-O-Gram 6: INTRODUCTION (INFORMAL)

group:_____

address:_____time:_____

title: DR. J. BRUCE WILSON

Time
(min.)

SCOOP: When our program chairman — Joe Harris — first assumed his present duties, he told us that he planned to schedule outstanding leaders of our community from all walks of life. He has done this most effectively and for today, representing public education, he has secured (see title).

JUMP-OFF: Recently, I asked a friend why he looked so depressed. "My future," he replied. "Why is it so hopeless?" etc.
Objective A: You can see by looking at our speaker that he is not depressed. The past has been good to him and he has made some excellent accomplishments. Certainly, with the start he has made, the future will deal well with him.
Objective B: Joe was unable to be with us today and he has asked me to introduce Dr. Wilson. I am delighted to have the opportunity.
Objective C: Let me tell you a little about the doctor, his youth and his career.
Promise: His talk will give all of us a

better understanding of the purposes and
functions of our junior college.

ADVANCE: (point 1) Dr. Wilson's latter
years are rich in educational experiences,
but I understand he had a little trouble
in the elementary grades.
Story: One day when he was ten, his father
asked him how he liked school. Bruce replied, "Closed!"
He learned the facts of life the
first day he went to school. When he re-
turned his mother was waiting at the door
to greet him, "Did you learn anything at
school today?" she asked eagerly. "You
bet I did," he said quickly. "All the kids
get an allowance but me."
He was born in Berryville, Arkansas,
in July, 1927, and graduated from Blythe-
ville High School (1946). He received the
A.A. degree at Northwest Mississippi Junior
College and the B.Ed. degree at Arkansas
State College. At the University of Florida
he earned the M.Ed. degree (1953) and the
D.Ed. degree (1955).

ADVANCE: (point 2) As we consider Dr.
Wilson's adult career, we find that he has
been a very successful man. His wife
LaVerne appreciates this and advised him
recently that a man is successful because
he has a wife to tell him what to do and
a secretary to do it for him.
Dr. Wilson has served in many important capacities: teacher, athletic director,
member Kellogg Leadership Staff, consultant
with Science Research Associates, Chicago,
Dean of Gulf Coast Community College and
first President of the Brevard Junior Col-

lege. He is an officer and member in many
important educational organizations, a
Kiwanian and author.

ASSAULT: Brevard County is most fortunate
in having Dr. Wilson serving in the important post of president of our new and
rapidly growing community junior college.
Likewise, our organization is most fortunate in having him with us today to talk
about our college.

MOP-UP: Now, it is my pleasure and privilege to present the distinguished president
of the new Brevard Junior College, Dr. J.
Bruce Wilson . . . Dr. Wilson.

Speech-O-Gram 7

PRESENTATION OF AWARD

Safety Behind the Scenes

The presentation of a cup or plaque needs careful wording to assure that suitable reference is made to the occasion and the achievements of the recipient. The talk must include comments that express good will on the part of those for whom the speaker speaks and must leave a feeling of genuine accomplishment on the part of the recipient. It is possible to include all of these objectives in the Speech-O-Gram. About fifteen minutes in length is adequate for this type of speech; a longer talk would be considered excessive.

Speech-O-Gram 7: PRESENTATION OF AWARD

group:_____

address:_____ time:_____

title: SAFETY BEHIND THE SCENES

Time
(min.)

SCOOP: Your president and I have been
talking about your company and the constant effort all of you have made to improve your safety record in the plant.
Therefore, in the few minutes I have
tonight, I will discuss (see title). I,
too, am concerned about safety. You see,
I'm in insurance and have worked closely
with your safety committee.

JUMP-OFF: The subject calls to mind the
story of the cub reporter who cut his
article to the bare essentials.
Objective A: This experience shows how
employee safety requires constant vigilance
— the kind your company has displayed and
the results of which have occasioned my
appearance here tonight.
Objective B: Actually, my principal purpose is to present an award, but accustomed
as I am to talking safety, I'll include
that too.
Objective C: First, I want to analyze your
company's progress in achieving an out-

standing safety record; then I will present
an award.
Promise: I hope I may inspire you to work
for even greater excellence in the future.

ADVANCE: (point 1) Consider first your
excellent safety record. What steps did
you take to attain it?
Story: (Tell story of the foreman who was
filling out papers on a casualty at the
factory where he worked.)

Your motives in establishing such a
program were humanitarian — you prevented
human suffering and saved lives, at the same
time you made certain financial gains.

The committee which guided your program deserves special mention: (name
membership).

Regular departmental inspections, a
sound, progressive, and highly imaginative
program and action taken by foremen and
executives in correcting hazardous conditions all added up to greater safety for
all employees.

Steps taken included: placing adhesive strips on stairways to prevent slips
and falls; instruction in use of fire-
fighting equipment; screening of fans;
improved parking arrangements — and many
others. It was an ambitious program; you
deserve high commendation.

ADVANCE: (point 2) Now, I am honored to
present this plaque attesting to your
achievements:

Whereas, the New Jersey Chemical
Laboratories have made a continuous and
concerted effort during the year 1961-62
to reduce safety hazards, and

Whereas, the results obtained have markedly reduced the number of accidents among employees; therefore,

Be it resolved, that the New Jersey Chemical Laboratories be highly commended for extraordinary results in plant safety.

This plaque is signed by J. Frank Strawbridge, General Insurance Casualty of New Jersey. (Presentation.)

ASSAULT: President Strawbridge regretted that he was unable to be with you tonight to present this award, but he asked me to tell you that the company is well aware of the noteworthy and extraordinary effort that has been made individually and collectively by your company.

MOP-UP: In closing, let me add my own congratulations. It has been a pleasure to review your successes and an honor to present the plaque. Someone — I think it was a woman — said, "A man is successful because he has a wife to tell him what to do and a secretary to do it for him." In this instance, however, you did it on your own.

Speech-O-Gram 8

ADDRESS TO BUSINESS EXECUTIVES

ROBOT EXECUTIVES—A Growing Threat to American Industry

Chambers of Commerce, management and sales executives, groups and large national organizations frequently call upon leaders in business to present their views on subjects related to their particular interests. The content of such talks fits easily into the pattern set by the Speech-O-Gram and its use eases the extra burden of preparing a speech. *"Robot Executives—A Growing Threat to American Industry"* was delivered by Mr. Louis E. Wolfson, President and Chairman of the Board, Merritt-Chapman & Scott Corporation, before the Sales Executive Council of the Louisville Chamber of Commerce (November 10, 1958) and served as a basis for this Speech-O-Gram. The complete speech, as originally written and published, is available upon request to Merritt-Chapman & Scott Corporation, 261 Madison Avenue, New York 16.

Speech-O-Gram 8: ADDRESS TO BUSINESS EXECUTIVES

group:_____

address:_____time:_____

title: ROBOT EXECUTIVES—
A Growing Threat to American Industry

Time
(min.)

SCOOP: Mr. White, your president, has been telling me about the excellent work you have been doing to sell young people on our traditional system of free enterprise and the American way of life. Your endeavors correlate perfectly with the purposes of my talk (see tile). Apparently, we are thinking together on this vital topic.

JUMP-OFF: It is appropriate that I read a letter received from the president of the New Enterprises Club of Harvard.
Objective A: This clear-thinking young man and his organization deplore the fact that while students have the ability and education to enter new enterprises, they are not doing this today. Apparently, there is a lack of motivation to pioneer, to create, to take a chance, to be enterprisers in the best sense of the word.
Objective B: Let us see what can be done to instill the missing urge and recapture the American pioneer spirit in our young people.
Objective C: Let us see who is to blame and what are the dangers. Then, we should examine the ingredients of industrial progress and the place of the individual within this framework. Lastly, let us look at what we,

as businessmen, can do to preserve and foster the pioneer spirit.

Promise: Such a discussion should make us more aware of a serious lack that faces America and encourage us to double our efforts in selling the American system of free enterprise.

ADVANCE: (point 1) First, consider the problems of conformity as it exists in business and its dangers for America.

Story: Mr. C. H. Greenewalt, president of E. I. du Pont de Nemours & Co., as reported in Business Week, emphasized that the cult of conformity, the subordination of self to the organization...must not be allowed to smother the identity of the individual executive.

A recent advertisement for research department personnel in The New York Times stated, "At Grumman (Aircraft Engineering Corporation) it is the individual engineer upon whom our company depends for its progress, particularly in the field of research. Grumman recognizes that competent research must allow for individual make-ups and temperaments if the creative process is to produce the results sought. This latitude for the individual is the key to research at Grumman."

Others awake to the dangers of conformity in many phases of our national life − politics, arts, education − include Dean Courtney C. Brown of Columbia University and Mr. William H. Whyte, Jr. of Fortune Magazine, who have written or spoken to the point on this matter.

ADVANCE: (point 2) The second consideration will be the ingredients of industrial progress and the place of the individual within the free enterprise system.

Progress has been built through trial and error. Latitude for the individual should be the rule.

Creative initiative is vital to success. Such untried ideas as auto sales on the installment plan, meat packaging, the assembly line, the concept of the supermarket, and prefabricated housing had tremendous impact.

Unless the individual is provided full opportunity to express himself, and encouraged to do so, majority rule can defeat its very purpose.

The creative thinker is vital to our economy.

ASSAULT: Young men with adventuring minds are not fools. If they see little scope for creative thinking and action in business, they will not enter it. Business must first establish a healthful climate and build tolerance for men with imagination.

Creative talent now available can be encouraged by every company. Business must seek out and sell itself to the brightest brains of coming generations. Business must see to it that the next generation of businessmen is adequately trained to shoulder its responsibilities. Selection methods need to be improved. Students seeking a business career should acquire a broad education.

MOP-UP: In closing, let me remind you that there are serious dangers in the present-day conformity we find in robot executives. America grew in strength as the result of creative genius of nonconformist individuals. The pioneer made America.

Speech-O-Gram 9

VALEDICTORY ADDRESS

Big Challenges

As surely as June rolls around, carefully selected graduates from schools at all levels settle down to the task of composing the valedictory address. The pattern for this type of speech is the same whether it is used in connection with a grade school, junior high school, high school, or college graduation. In *Big Challenges,* elements include the recall of certain events, the recitation of benefits, and an expression of gratitude. After recapturing the past, the speaker goes on to show how gains made by the group will help in the accomplishment of future goals. The valedictorian speaks for the class, using "we" rather than "I" throughout. The speech is warm, friendly, inspirational and brief.

Speech-O-Gram 9: VALEDICTORY ADDRESS

group:_____

address:_____time:_____

title: BIG CHALLENGES

Time
(min.)

SCOOP: Mr. Rath has said that our big challenges lie ahead of us. Even now, I wouldn't argue with our principal. In fact, I've chosen to speak on (see title). Nonetheless, we all remember our early days at Coral Gables High School.

JUMP-OFF: All of us will recall the time Judd Haley came into study hall, etc.
Objective A: Many suffered embarrassment, difficulty, even pain during that first year and afterwards. We worked, we laughed, we learned. Put it all together and the result is preparation for what's ahead.
Objective B: Let's look at the benefits of these experiences, be grateful for them and look forward.
Objective C: The principal considerations will be:
        Educational benefits — the gains we were seeking.
        Physical and moral benefits — the extras we found.
Promise: As Miss Snure used to say in

English class, "A review won't hurt; in
fact, it might help us remember."

ADVANCE: (point 1) First, let us consider
the educational aspects of our three years
at Coral Gables High School.
Story: One day a teacher asked the fellow
behind me, "Why don't you answer me?"
          "I did, Mr. Stroup. I shook my
head."
          "But," said Mr. Stroup, "you don't
expect me to hear your head rattle way up
here?"
          That's just kidding. Actually, we
learned much from our teachers. They were
patient, kind and helpful and we shall remember them always with deep gratitude.
          The knowledge we gained under their
tutelage will stand us in good stead wher-
ever we go, giving us confidence, a feeling
of adequacy, a desire for more knowledge.
          Elbert Hubbard said, "The object of
teaching a child is to enable him to get
along without his teacher." We are no
longer children, but we are better able to
stand alone academically in a world where
a good education is vital.

ADVANCE: (point 2) Next, consider the
physical and moral gains of the past three
years — those privileges we had on the
basketball, tennis, volleyball courts and
the football fields; in the debate society;
in our service clubs.
          What grand opportunities we had to
practice good sportsmanship, to learn self-
discipline, control, cooperation and to
exert initiative.
          H. J. van Dyke said, "The true object

of education should be to train one to
think clearly and act rightly."
        Our years at Gables gave us all of
this and much more, and we are most
grateful.

ASSAULT: We know there are big challenges
ahead of us: the Communist threat, moral
rearmament, peace uses of the atom, a trip
to the moon — to name a few. We intend to
meet these and many more big challenges
in our time. The excellent training we
received at Gables has given us a solid
rock upon which to build our confidence,
and through which to obtain good results.

MOP-UP: We will all long remember our
happy, productive years at Coral Gables
High School — our principal, the teachers,
the educational experiences afforded us,
the physical and moral gains. The memory
of these pleasant years, together with
their strengthening effects, will go with
us as we face the big challenge of tomorrow.

Speech-O-Gram 10

INSTALLATION

Dedicated Leadership

The installation speech contains three principal ingredients: an expression of appreciation for the appointment, recognition of the work of the preceding officer, and an indication as to major emphases during the speaker's tenure of office. A review of *Dedicated Leadership* will reveal that these factors have been included in the Speech-O-Gram. At the same time, informative and inspirational material has been included on qualities of leadership and their development in young people—a subject highly suited to this luncheon-club audience.

Speech-O-Gram 10: INSTALLATION

group:_____

address:_____time:_____

title: DEDICATED LEADERSHIP

Time
(min.)

SCOOP: Thanks, Bill, for those kind words, and thank you, gentlemen, for entrusting me with the presidency of the association. We all know that this post requires (see title) and I have decided to talk briefly on that subject tonight.

JUMP-OFF: (Tell story of how Junior went to the head of his class.)
<u>Objective A:</u> Junior's efforts were fine, but they didn't go far enough.

In every area — government, business, industry, education — there is a shortage of dedicated leadership, of people with ability who are willing workers, strong leaders.
<u>Objective B:</u> Therefore, let's look for a definition of leadership and determine whether it can be developed.
<u>Objective C:</u> The important points of discussion will be:

Qualities of leadership; and

The development of young leaders in our democracy.

136

<u>Promise:</u> Having considered these matters,
techniques may be learned that will help
in the training of younger fellows for jobs
requiring leadership.

ADVANCE: <u>(point 1)</u> First, consider qualities of leadership: what are they?
<u>Story:</u> The boss said to his secretary, "You
should have been here at 9 o'clock." "Why?"
she asked. "You've missed your coffee
break."

"The man who does his work, any work,
conscientiously, must always be in one
sense a great man." — Mulock.

But there is much more to effective
leadership than just work.

West Point definition: Leadership is
the art of influencing and directing people
to an assigned goal in such a manner as
to command their obedience, confidence,
respect and loyal cooperation.

In my book, the ingredients include
knowledge and the ability to apply it,
ability to understand and work with people,
insistence on high standards, ability to
inspire action and to communicate effectively through speech and writing.

ADVANCE: <u>(point 2)</u> Second, let us consider how leadership ability can be developed in America's young men.

Skeptics may say that people are born
to lead, that the quality cannot be developed. This is false.

Read Booton Herndon's <u>Young Men Can
Change the World.</u> Learn about George H.
Olmsted, Clifford D. Cooper, Paul D. Bag-
well, and other young men who became outstanding leaders.

If young men can profit by an education; if they can learn that other people
have egos too; if they will set high standards for themselves and others; if they
will learn to communicate, then they can
become leaders.

ASSAULT: As long as I can remember, our
club has been interested in the advance-
ment of young people. We have awarded
scholarships, conducted oratory contests
and sponsored a Boy Scout troop. Our past
president, Bill Harris, has done an outstanding job, leading our club to excellence in these endeavors. It is my hope
that I can measure up, in every respect,
to his stature as a leader.

MOP-UP: Before I close, let me tell you
once more how much I appreciate the confidence you have reposed in me. Also, let
me say that I believe much can be done to
build qualities of leadership (knowledge,
ability, understanding, high standards and
ability to communicate) in young people.
This club can help, and I shall do all in
my power to further the task.

Speech-O-Gram 11

INTRODUCTION AND CHARGE

Kenneth Rast Williams

When a person assumes the position of president of an institution, it is fitting that he be given a formal charge in which he is told the expectations of the governing body. This is normally preceded by an introduction which explains the man's qualifications for the post. Since the occasion is formal, humorous materials are omitted. Twenty minutes is a suitable length for such a talk.

Speech-O-Gram 11: INTRODUCTION AND CHARGE

group:_____

address:_____time:_____

title: KENNETH RAST WILLIAMS

Time
(min.)

SCOOP: Someone once said that there are two reasons for one's actions — a good one and a real one. My good reason for being here is to introduce (see title). My real reason is to tell him what he must do in his new job as president of our new junior college. I am honored to have both missions.

JUMP-OFF: Great achievement demands giving many years of life itself: e.g., Vergil, Dr. Williams, Webster.
Objective A: I'm certain that as relatives, friends and students of Dr. Williams, you feel a close kinship and believe you are well acquainted with him. We're all interested in people; today, especially, we're interested in knowing more about Dr. Williams.
Objective B: My purpose is to trace through the years for you; perhaps, in his busy life, he managed some extras you didn't know about.
Objective C: Let me tell you about his education, his service as an educator, his governmental posts, and the many honors which have been bestowed upon him during his lifetime. Then, I will present the charge.

140

Promise: I'm certain you will be amazed
that one man could accomplish as much as
Dr. Williams has in a relatively short
span of time. After hearing the details
of his background, you will know him
better.

ADVANCE: (point 1) Kenneth Rast Williams,
born in Monticello, Florida, October 26,
1908, the son of Dr. and Mrs. John Franklin
Williams. (Give list of schools and
degrees.)
Story: Dr. Williams has taught and held
administrative positions at all levels of
education. At the University of Georgia, he
was Assistant Professor of Education, Dean
of Students, and Dean of the College of
Education. He was Professor of School Administration at the University of Florida
from 1941-1943, and held various Air Force
training posts through 1946. In Atlanta,
he served as Consultant to the Board of
Education, and as Deputy Superintendent.
He was the first president of the Central
Florida Junior College. In addition to his
splendid record of service as a professional educator, Dr. Williams has held
numerous important governmental posts
(list). His professional activities are
many. He is a member of many civic, educational and honorary organizations. He is a
Rotarian and is listed in Who's Who in
America.

ADVANCE: (point 2) I am honored to present
the charge to Dr. Williams. Would you all
please stand? Dr. Williams, many dedicated
citizens have devoted thought, time and
effort to establish in our county a two-
year college which would provide higher

education for many young and older adults. The foresight and vision of these men and women finally led to the founding of the institution which you now head, and it is their cherished hope that the students who enter these halls of learning will gain academically, and be strengthened in personal adequacy, thereby increasing their usefulness in their community and their nation. Further, it is their desire that these students prepare to meet the conflicts, the vast social changes and the tremendous challenges which face us today and which will continue to plague our world in the autumn years of this century.

ASSAULT: And now, under the authority vested in me by the Governor of the State of Florida and the State Board of Education, and as a member of the Dade County Board of Public Instruction, it is my duty to charge you, Dr. Kenneth Rast Williams, with the responsibility of carrying out this tremendous task, with the help of God, as expeditiously and as effectively as it is within human power so to do. As you go about your tasks, keep in mind the aspirations of those men and women who were instrumental in the founding of the Dade County Junior College.

MOP-UP: All of us here today who have in one way or another helped to make the institution a reality — and all who will contribute to its future resources, traditions, accomplishments and its stature in the community, the state and the nation — wish you much success in your endeavors. May God speed you in your good works.

Speech-O-Gram 12

POLITICAL ENDORSEMENT

Rutherford (Rug) Haynes
Candidate for State Legislature

Occasionally, a speaker is called upon to speak in behalf of a political candidate. The Speech-O-Gram which has been developed on Rutherford (Rug) Haynes, candidate for State Legislature, is presented for the purpose of showing how a plea for political endorsement by a political organization might be organized. With slight adjustments, this material can be altered to serve as a nominating speech. Such a talk must include the following: naming the candidate and the position he seeks; description of the office to be filled; a statement of the qualifications of the candidate; a definite nomination of the candidate for the job. It will be noted that in this sample talk Rutherford (Rug) Haynes' name is mentioned twelve times. This is good politics, helping to fix it in the minds of the voters.

Speech-O-Gram 12: POLITICAL ENDORSEMENT

group:_____

address:_____time:_____

title: RUTHERFORD (RUG) HAYNES
Candidate for State Legislature

Time
(min.)

SCOOP: Your president — Josh Randell — has told me that your club wants a firsthand look-listen at candidates before making endorsements. A fine idea. I took a look-listen at (see title) and am certain you will be as favorably impressed as I am.

JUMP-OFF: Story of the gubernatorial candidate who stopped at a farmhouse.
Objective A: Like the farmer, "Rug" Haynes is a Democrat. His father and his grandfather were Democrats. He plans that all his sons will be Democrats. He is a candidate for the State Legislature and prays for your endorsement.
Objective B: It is our hope that my remarks and his will help you to make a decision favorable to "Rug."
Objective C: I want to discuss: personal qualifications and experience which equips "Rug" Haynes for the post he seeks. He intends to tell you of his plans, once he is elected.

144

<u>Promise:</u> After you have learned the facts and heard him speak, I know your decision in his favor will come easily.

ADVANCE: <u>(point 1)</u> First, let us consider the personal qualifications of Rutherford (Rug) Haynes.
<u>Story:</u> Bryant said once, "Difficulty is the nurse of greatness."

"Difficulty": this is the "Rug" Haynes story. He was born in our town thirty-three years ago, the son of a poor, hard-working millhand. "Rug" went to work early in life, earning his own way, staying in school in spite of tremendous financial handicaps. He graduated from Harvard High School and went on to State U., where he supported himself while studying law. He graduated in 1952. Since then, he has practiced law over in Middleton, where he lives with his wife and four sons.

ADVANCE: <u>(point 2)</u> Our second consideration will be Rutherford (Rug) Haynes' experience in elective office.

Someone said, "The statesman wishes to steer, while the politician is satisfied to drift."

"Rug" started his political career as judge of the small claims court and brought about many needed reforms.

He did a fine job and the voters reëlected him at the close of his first term.

He was elected circuit judge three years ago and has served the people admirably ever since, not as a politician but as a statesman.

ASSAULT: Rutherford (Rug) Haynes is a
candidate for the State Legislature — an
office which requires honesty, sincerity,
experience, initiative, a willingness to
work, and a close acquaintance with our
local community. We need a statesman — one
who steers and does not drift. Such a man
is "Rug" Haynes.

MOP-UP: I am about to close, but let me
point out again that "Rug" was born and
raised right here in our own community.
He came up the hard way, as many of us did.
He worked to become a well-qualified attorney. He has gained political experience,
having served as judge in the small claims
and circuit courts. Rutherford (Rug)
Haynes will serve well. He deserves your
endorsement.

Speech-O-Gram 13

CLUB TALK

Crime Books and Juvenile Delinquency

An informative talk on some aspect of the lives of children can always hold the attention of parents. The speech on crime books and juvenile delinquency is one that would be suitable for presentation before a PTA group, a fathers' club or a civic club.

group:_____

address:_____time:_____

title: CRIME BOOKS AND JUVENILE DELINQUENCY

Time
(min.)

SCOOP: Your program chairman told me of your recent discussions of and concern for juvenile delinquency. For that reason, I decided to talk on (see title). I have three young sons myself and am concerned about their behavior and what they read.

JUMP-OFF: Story of twelve delinquent youths and the judge who sentenced them: "We're not treating you like kids any longer. . . ."

Objective A: But were these youths treated like "kids" in the first place? Were they protected against the corrupting influence of comic books which glamorize and advertise knives and guns capable of being rigged into deadly weapons?

Objective B: My purpose is to give you facts about crime "comic" books, and to show their effects on children.

Objective C: Primary points of concern will be the content of these fast-selling items and what it does to young minds.

Promise: With these facts in mind you may decide to take action . . . constructive action that will save you and your family much grief and will help to raise the moral standards of children everywhere.

ADVANCE: (point 1) First, let me make
ou fully aware of the kind of ideas pre-
_ented in these books.
Story: One comic-book story begins with a
"hood" giving advice to two little boys:
"If you kids wanna learn to be like me,
you gotta be tough! Never give the other
guy an even break!"

The "hood" shows them a well-dressed
young boy. They proceed to threaten this
boy and he hands over his money. But that
does not satisfy their tough teacher. He
bangs their heads together and exclaims,
"You always have to slug 'em! Remember
that." This, parents, is the elementary
lesson of crime comic books.

Some adults think they know all about
crime comic books. They've read mystery
and detective novels. But reports given
by the Lafargue Clinic show that parents
have only a vague conception of these
books. Children know what they're all
about. When available, they read them
avidly, digesting each choice tidbit.

ADVANCE: (point 2) The second consideration is this: the effect of crime comics
on the thoughts of children.

(Tell story of the city boy who
visited his uncle's farm.)

The child learns from doing and
reading.

Josette Frank in Our Children Today
asks, "Will children, exposed to the pic-
tured portrayal of violence . . . be
damaged or confused or frightened by them?"
Her answer is in the affirmative.

Dr. Frederic Wertham in his book
Seduction of the Innocent pointed out:
"The average parent has no idea that every

imaginable crime is described in detail in comic books."

We take pride in the ability of our children to read; but, because books put ideas in people's heads, we must direct our children toward fine books.

ASSAULT: Prior to the era of comic books, few serious crimes were committed by children. But in 1959, police arrests of children under eighteen in the U.S. (1,789 cities of 2,500 or more population) was 320,669. In 1960, four times as many children were sentenced to Federal prisons as in 1940.

Dr. Wertham tells of many atrocities committed by children well-read in comic books: "A fourteen-year-old crime-comics addict killed a fourteen-year-old girl by stabbing her thirteen times with a knife. He did not know her." He tells of many such happenings. His book is <u>must</u> reading for everyone.

MOP-UP: I must close now, but let me reiterate: These books contain filth, corruption, meanness and intrigue — they can have only an adverse effect on the mind of the child who reads them.

As parents we must strive to raise the level of the literary tastes of our children and broaden their interests in right directions.

You can help your children and your community if you will take positive steps, show an interest in what your children read, and introduce them to the treasury of fine books in your public library.

Speech-O-Gram 14

COMMENCEMENT ADDRESS

Master Keys to Tomorrow

High-school graduates want lively commencement addresses, and they prefer them to be short. High school seniors and even the more sophisticated college students like these talks to be direct, personal and inspirational, but not overly serious. Fifteen minutes is adequately long for any robed and captive group of teen-agers who want to get it over with as soon as possible.

Speech-O-Gram 14: COMMENCEMENT ADDRESS

group:_____

address:_____time:_____

title: MASTER KEYS TO TOMORROW

Time
(min.)

SCOOP: Your Principal — Mr. Rath — told me that you graduates are eager to get on to college or into a job. Realizing this, I decided to talk on (see title). You need to know how to get your foot in the right door ...fast. I am all that stands between you and the diploma which will allow this, so I'll make it short.

JUMP-OFF: There is the story of a man who had always longed to be the captain of a ship.
<u>Objective A:</u> As adults you will need to do more than just wear a captain's cap. You must make tangible contributions, and you will need the attitudes that make this possible. Although you are having an exciting and memorable experience tonight, I know that you wish to find solid ground as you enter the adult world.
<u>Objective B:</u> I hope to inspire at least a few of you to make the extra effort required for top achievement.
<u>Objective C:</u> Let's look at you and your attitudes first; then, find out how you can

152

make your work count for something important.

Promise: Once your basic attitudes are on
firm ground, you will be able to establish
constructive goals and move rapidly to the
successful achievements and work satisfac-
tions you desire.

ADVANCE: (point 1) First, consider your
"internal" attitudes: what you must be like
inside to move confidently into adulthood
and toward successful achievement.
Story: A beautiful, healthy young lady told
me the other day that, with things as they
are in the world, she felt that effort to be
successful was a waste of time. You and I
know that her attitude was wrong.

Harry Emerson Fosdick said, "Nobody
ever finds life worth living. One always has
to make it worth living." Helen Keller did
that. Born deaf, dumb, and blind, she made
a great adjustment for her lack of sensory
perceptions. She developed abilities which
made her handicaps seem almost a reward.

Alice, a young girl I know, is making
her life worth living. She was set on getting through college. She wanted to help
others who were handicapped like herself.
She made it in spite of physical and financial handicaps. Now she is teaching children
who are crippled with spastic paralysis.
Alice did not find life worth living; she
made it so.

ADVANCE: (point 2) The second point to remember is that of making efforts count.

Bismarck said, "To youth I have but
three words of counsel — work, work, work!"

Some people spend most of their time
and effort trying to avoid work. At 10:30,

when his new steno arrived for work, the
boss said, "You should have been here at
nine o'clock."

"Why?" she asked, "what happened?"

Instead of settling down to hard work
and obvious accomplishment, we dawdle and
try to find the easy way. An employer asked
one of his men, "How come you're carrying
only one sack? All the others are carrying
two."

"Gee whiz, Boss," said the worker,
"guess the other guys are too lazy to make
two trips like I do."

ASSAULT: Too many of us are like Jerome K.
Jerome, who said in his book <u>Three Men in a
Boat,</u> "I like work; it fascinates me. I can
sit and look at it for hours."

Many are afraid of a tough job; we
fear failure and never try. A successful
salesman I know calls on the toughest cus-
tomers. I asked him once how he gets in the
mood for the rough guys. He explained, "I say
to myself: Where am I? I'm out here. Where
is he? In there. Where do I have to go? In
there where he is. What if he says no and
tosses me out — where am I then? Out here —
where I am now. I've got nothing to lose!"
That man has the right attitude.

MOP-UP: Now, just before you receive your
diplomas, let me say again: Establish right
attitudes toward work; want success and be
willing to work toward great achievement.

"Nothing is impossible to a man who
can will, and then do; this is the only law
of success."

Longfellow said, "The talent of success is nothing more than doing what you can
do well; and doing well whatever you do."

Speech-O-Gram 15

ADDRESS TO INDUSTRIAL LEADERS

Plant Location

Approximately 3200 trade, business and commercial organizations (everything from the American Institute of Certified Public Accountants to the American Zinc Institute) are listed in the *Encyclopedia of American Associations* (Gale Research Co., Detroit, 1959, 2nd ed.). Many of these organizations bring their membership together annually for meetings in our larger cities. As every business man and woman knows almost too well, the principal means of communication—except for some fast repartee over a late afternoon cocktail—is the public speech. Leaders in these organizations are frequently called upon to speak at sectional meetings or to the entire assembly, and it is important that they project a favorable image of their company. The Speech-O-Gram will be helpful to both the experienced speaker and the beginner as they strive to present their ideas with forcible fluency from the floor of the convention.

group:_____

address:_____time:_____

Title: PLANT LOCATION

Time
(min.)

SCOOP: Governor Smith has told me about a problem of yours which in my estimation should solve itself with great ease — that is, to bring new industry to the state. You have addressed yourself to a major topic of the day; I will do the same as I talk on (see title). It is good to be wanted. As a businessman, you have warmed my heart.

JUMP-OFF: The occasion brings to mind the story of the roomer who was unable to remember his landlady's name.
<u>Objective A:</u> This incident proves that there are right and wrong ways to accomplish one's ends.

Industry is looking for certain things as it seeks new locations.

The climate needs to be right for the company.

The company needs to be right for the community.
<u>Objective B:</u> Therefore, let's look for ways to bring companies to this state instead of sitting back and watching them go to other states.

Objective C: Important considerations will
be physical factors, community attitudes
toward the type of organization and industry, and the possibility of profitable
economic performance in the community.
Promise: A discussion of these basic factors
will give you an understanding of the many
factors placed in balance as a company makes
the difficult decision as to plant location.

ADVANCE: (point 1) Let us consider first
the physical factors and community attitudes toward the new company.
Story: Industry has not always found the
welcome mat waiting at a city's doorstep.
    Gwilym A. Price, Chairman and Presi-
dent of Westinghouse Electric Corporation,
in a speech entitled "The Climate That Industry Seeks," compared the attitude to
that of a European woman who was distressed
at the large number of Americans who were
thronging her country. "Why," she demanded,
"can't they stay home and just send over
the money?"
    New companies are no longer inter-
lopers if the choice is made after careful
study by an experienced plant-locating
committee.
    Physical factors include everything
from pleasant living conditions for employees' families to educational and trans-
portation facilities.
    Attitudes looked for include: whole-
hearted acceptance, community understanding,
and continuing fair treatment.

ADVANCE: (point 2) Next, let us consider
the vital concern over profitable economic
performance.
    Leonard C. Yaseen in his book Plant
Location (American Research Council, N. Y.,

1960) points out that: "Industry is expand-
ing and relocating because of shifting
markets, steadily mounting freight costs,
the need for new labor reservoirs, the
desire to operate in low-cost small com-
munities, and the requirement for new
straight-line production facilities."

The locating of the plant is two-
sided. Management's effect on the community
is favorable if it is productive and profitable. The community needs to make this possible or else the partnership fails.

ASSAULT: Your state has made tremendous
strides toward bringing companies here.
(Cite examples and mention responsible
individuals.) The profit motive, operating
as it does in America, strengthens the local
community and the nation. As Winston
Churchill said, "It is a socialist idea
that making profits is a vice; I consider
the real vice is making losses." And to
quote Bernard Baruch, "Unless each man
produces more than he receives, increases
his output, there will be less for him and
all the others."

MOP-UP: In closing, let us review the factors involved in plant location:

Physical factors must include pleasant
living conditions for employees, good
streets, parks, schools, transporation
facilities.

Community atitudes must be favorable
to the company.

Possibilities for economic success
must be favorable or the partnership fails.

Story about Max, the marriage broker,
who took his client to look over a certain
female prospect.

Speech-O-Gram 16

SALES TALK

The Bird Watcher's Pac

The sales talk must be carefully handled to obtain favorable results. Naturally, at the beginning it is necessary to get the attention of the listener. After that, it is mainly a matter of pointing out the advantage, proving that advantage, and urging the prospect to grasp it. As a final step, the salesman asks for an order. The format of the Speech-O-Gram is suited to this plan of presentation and assists in assuring that all the basic aspects of selling are included. This talk was designed for presentation before a bird-watchers club.

Speech-O-Gram 16: SALES TALK

group:_____

address:_____time:_____

title: THE BIRD WATCHER'S PAC

Time
(min.)

SCOOP: Mrs. Sullivan, our hostess, has told me that everyone here tonight is interested in bird watching, but that many of you do not own suitable equipment. As a bird watcher myself I know that the right equipment is essential and I am prepared to provide you with (see title).

JUMP-OFF: A friend of mine missed a chance to watch the quetzal in Central America last summer.
Objective A: Such experiences prove the advantage of always being properly equipped for this wonderful year-round sport. And, obviously, the better we can see the bird, the more rewarding the effort.
Objective B: Therefore, let's look for ways to provide each of you with at least the basic requirements for successful bird watching.
Objective C: I want to discuss the items needed and show the advantages of owning the new Bird Watcher's Pac.
Promise: I think that once you learn about

this convenient and inexpensive equipment
you will decide never to be without it.

ADVANCE: (point 1) First, let us consider
what you need for a more successful bird
watching trip.
Story: The other day I dropped into an
antique shop. Feeling in a jovial mood I
said to the proprietor, "What's new?" "Not
a thing," he said. "I like old things."
        Well, The Bird Watcher's Pac is new.
True, old things are fine, until the new
things are better. The convenient carrying
case of durable cowhide contains your
binoculars, field guide, a set of 25 pocket
field cards suited to this area, a field
notebook and three pencils for record keeping. Everything fits neatly into the compact case, complete with partitions for
each item and a comfortable carrying handle.
        The bird glasses may be had in any
standard magnification, field and illumina-
tion. They are the center-focusing models
preferred for birding because of the ease
and speed in adjusting for range.

ADVANCE: (point 2) Next, consider the obvious advantages of owning this convenient
and complete packet of equipment.
        Most important, your wonderful hobby
will be enhanced because many new facets
will be added. Your enjoyment in watching
will be greater because of the magnification. With your binoculars and the other
equipment, it will be like listening to
stereophonic sound instead of one-track
reproduction. You will be able to identify
birds more readily, help with bird censuses,
study bird migrations and their behavior in

the natural habitat. Once you have watched
birds through satisfactory binoculars, you
will never be without them again.

ASSAULT: This item is not available on the
open market. In fact, you can purchase it
only from district representatives of the
Apex Equipment Co., who visit you personally as I am doing tonight. The entire kit
is guaranteed; the binoculars you receive
will be in perfect adjustment and free from
defects. Our company has been established
in Boston for seventy-five years and can
furnish repair parts and complete service.
After a thirty-day trial period, you may
return the set for a full cash refund. As
an extra bonus, I am going to include a
long-playing record which will help you
recognize and remember bird songs.

MOP-UP: I have listed the equipment you
need for enjoyable and successful bird
watching and showed you the advantages in
owning the items contained in the complete
and compact Bird Watcher's Pac. Why not step
into new enjoyment of your wonderful hobby,
place your order with me tonight — right
now — and get the free bird record? I know
you will never regret your decision.

Speech-O-Gram 17

ADDRESS TO GOVERNMENTAL COMMITTEE

Preparing Students for College

The speaker may be called upon to present a talk before a governmental committee as was the situation for this talk. Dr. J. Bruce Wilson, a college president, was asked to talk before the Committee on Quality Education which had been called upon to investigate education in the state and render a report to the Governor, the State Board of Education and the Legislature. An instructional and highly inspirational speech was prepared, the Speech-O-Gram of which follows.

Speech-O-Gram 17: ADDRESS TO GOVERNMENTAL COMMITTEE

group:_____

address:_____time:_____

title: PREPARING STUDENTS FOR COLLEGE

Time
(min.)

SCOOP: Your chairman has told me that your purpose is to investigate all phases of education, grades 1 through 12. He suggested that I talk on (see title). All of us here today have similar interests. You see, as a college president, I must deal with the products of the public schools.

JUMP-OFF: (Tell story about the wise high-school boy who said to the bus driver, "Well, Noah, you finally got here," etc.) Objective A: Colleges are bulging today. Most of them are not out looking for students; on the contrary, they are screening them out. Our students need to find out early what they want to do with their lives; we need to assist them in the learning process, and to measure results. Objective B: I'll discuss college requirements and suggest educational pillars which must be strengthened to help our children prepare for college. Objective C: Chief considerations will be:

capabilities of teachers, physical facilities and instructional tools.
Promise: By studying these aspects of education, this committee will strike at the
very structures that determine quality
teaching and quality learning.

ADVANCE: (point 1) First, consider the goal
toward which many of the students are being
directed: namely, college-level work.
Story: At least, that is where many parents
hope to put their children after they graduate from high school. (Tell story about
p-u-t and p-u-t-t.)

Many parents want to put their children in college. Their reasons are many.
Whatever these may be, the job for the student is essentially the same and the drop-
out is heavy.

More and more students are entering
college. Qualified students can get into
college today. There is room for everyone,
but....

Benefits are many and qualified students should be encouraged to attend.

About half of the young people who
enter college finally graduate. The reason
for drop-outs: lack of essential training.
Successful students attended schools with
highly capable teachers, much homework,
strong guidance program, modern teaching
equipment, a well-organized curriculum.

ADVANCE: (point 2) Our second consideration
will be three pillars of quality in education: Teachers, schoolrooms and teaching
tools.

Good teaching requires good teachers.
The average salary for teachers in Florida

in 1958 was $4,971; in Alaska that year it
was $6,546; in California, $6,010. Teaching
is a steady job. The cost of living index
may go up, but a teacher's salary remains
steady. Florida has a classroom shortage.
In 1960, we had 73,000 too many students.
We needed 5,000 more classrooms. Inventors
have prepared better teaching tools — motion
pictures, slides, educational TV — but
they're not getting rich. School budgets
are close. Seldom are bright, new teaching
machines budgeted.

ASSAULT: We must continue to bring in
teachers with highest capabilities, improve
physical facilities and instructional tools.
    Our future depends upon our educa-
tional system. Our people must be willing
to accept only the best; recognize that we
are in a technical and scientific race with
Communism; re-examine values: education vs.
peanuts, cosmetics, liquor and weight-
reducing pills. Our people need to determine
if a living wage is related to the recruit-
ment of good teachers.

MOP-UP: As I close, let me say again:
Students need to set their sights early and
work in the direction of a college education, if that is their goal.
    We can best assist them in doing this
if we will improve conditions for teachers,
provide more classroom stations and better
teaching tools.
    We need to evaluate continually our
educational system and to act on our find-
ings. Drastic steps will be required to
improve teaching and learning that lives
up to the needs of America today.

Speech-O-Gram 18

BUSINESS CONVENTION

Business and Higher Education—The Vital Link

The training of young executives is a topic of considerable interest to leading businessmen because of industry's need for properly qualified executives. The Speech-O-Gram as presented for this subject is informative and persuasive and suitable for presentation as a convention speech to any large business organization at convention time.

Speech-O-Gram 18: BUSINESS CONVENTION

group:_____

address:_____time:_____

title: BUSINESS AND HIGHER EDUCATION—
THE VITAL LINK

Time
(min.)

SCOOP: Ladies and gentlemen, your chairman has told me that one of your chief concerns today is thorough training for young executives. I, too, want them well-qualified and have decided to talk on (see title). You see, I am in higher education and the monkey is on my back as much as it is on yours.

JUMP-OFF: Several years ago, Mr. Harvey S. Firestone specified the kind of background he wanted for young executives.
Objective A: His views are agreeable to me and to many business leaders today. But it places a burden on the colleges. They must live up to the challenge and the confidence expressed by corporation executives.
Objective B: Therefore, let us look for ways and means of assisting higher education and help it do a better job.
Objective C: First, let us discuss what kind of educational training leading businessmen expect young executives to have; and, second, what businessmen must do to assure in the future a goodly supply of well-trained young men for managerial positions.

Promise: By facing the matter squarely, you
will become better acquainted with trends
and be prepared to meet the requirements of
the future.

ADVANCE: (point 1) First, the matter of
training: What does business need and want
from its young executives?
Story: The U. S. Chamber of Commerce reports
that the council on financial aid to education recently checked the educational
background of the top 200 officials of the
nation's 100 largest manufacturing concerns.
A total of 173, or 86.5 per cent had attended college. In 1953, the comparable
figure was 75 per cent.

The survey showed that of the 173 who
had attended colleges, 143 (or 70 per cent)
graduated.

The Chamber states that "colleges and
universities...are the farm clubs for business executives."

Apparently, business management is
going in the same direction as the law,
medicine and teaching professions.

There is a close tie between the need
for business leadership, and higher education. Obviously, if businessmen expect a
quality education for their people, they
cannot afford to take a do-nothing attitude
toward higher education.

ADVANCE: (point 2) Second, the role of
business: What must be done to assure a continuing supply of educationally able young
executives?

During the current year, business and
industry have supported higher education to
the tune of $150 million.

College enrollments are increasing

rapidly. Whereas 598,000 students attended
institutions of higher learning in 1920, in
1956 there were 2,996,000 — almost five
times as many — and now the figure is climb-
ing faster than ever.

According to the Chamber of Commerce,
the $150 million will have to be increased
several times to keep abreast with the
swelling enrollments — $500 million in 1970.

This is where you — the leaders in
American business — come in.

ASSAULT: You must plan to give five times
as much voluntary support to the colleges
and universities as you have in the past.
Your organizations will need to join the
growing parade of businesses which donate
regularly to this purpose — firms like
Standard Oil Co. of New Jersey, headed by
M. J. Rathbone, President. This company
pioneered in corporate giving to colleges.
In the past five years, Jersey Standard
forked over $9.5 million to 494 schools.

Let's face it: business leaders have
become increasingly dependent on higher
education and the system of higher education cannot run effectively without money.

MOP-UP: I am about to close, but first let
me point out that business leaders today
are requiring more and more training for
their executives. They are not satisfied
with four years of undergraduate training;
now they are asking for the master's and
doctor's degrees. Graduate training is ex-
pensive, and — to use an old cliché — "you
can't get something for nothing." You know
this. So make your plans. Lend your principal support to the colleges and universities.

Speech-O-Gram 19

AFTER-DINNER SPEECH

Female vs. Male Drivers

This is a talk on safe driving designed for presentation as an after-dinner speech. The purpose is to entertain and, at the same time, gently urge driving safety. The speaker is a woman and the audience, male.

Speech-O-Gram 19: AFTER-DINNER SPEECH

group:_____

address:_____time:_____

title: FEMALE vs. MALE DRIVERS

Time
(min.)

SCOOP: I learned from your chairman that practically everyone here is married and owns two cars. This fact makes it doubly important that I talk with you on (see title). You gentlemen probably have decided that you are the better drivers. But, hold your decision — I've been to the library.

JUMP-OFF: (Tell story about the lady who drove her car into a tree; story of the beatnik who backed out of driveway.)
Objective A: Such experiences prove that men and women have their problems when it comes to driving cars. Both sexes need to improve in their ability to drive, and they need to be more careful.
Objective B: Methods used by the lady and the Beat were wrong. Let's look for another way to get the Caddy into the garage and surely there is a better way to tame a dog.
Objective C: First, let's see if we can settle the argument over who are the best drivers; and, second, look for ways to improve everyone's safety record.

172

<u>Promise</u>: Perhaps our discussion will help
you find a good argument to use when your
wife back-seat drives; or, maybe teach you
not to make mistakes which bring on the
criticisms.

ADVANCE: <u>(point 1)</u> First, let us consider
that threadbare argument comparing women
drivers and men drivers.
<u>Story</u>: There was a scatterbrained young lady
who got a $1.00 parking ticket and then dis-
covered the meter was broken — ended up
paying $10.00 fine.

Mother reported her car stolen — then
she remembered she left it parked downtown.
Yes, women do have minor faults. They try
to take advantage of the fact that they are
women, and expect special treatment. They
are timid, short in stature and lack
strength. They are poor judges of distance and panic easily. They try to talk
and drive at the same time. This is bad,
especially when they gesture with both
hands.

Men aren't much to brag about, either.
(Tell story of the young fellow in his
sports car.) Men drivers take chances, they
show off, they try to make like Jim Rathmann
on the Indianapolis Speedway. Women have a
slight edge statistically, but the argument
isn't important; improvement counts.

ADVANCE: <u>(point 2)</u> Let us consider some
of the ways we can cut back on the crashes.

I could say, "Don't drink while driving." None of you here would do that, but
some people still do. They take the attitude
of the drunk in the gutter who was told by
a lady passer-by that alcohol was bad —

very bad. "I wouldn't drink it if they gave
it away," she said. He lay there, unable to
get up, and finally muttered, "If you ain't
tried the stuff, don't knock it."

I could say, "Don't speed." But then
they build cars to go 120 m.p.h. and you
feel you've got to get your money's worth.

I could say, "Be careful, when driving." But I don't want to be a spoilsport.

ASSAULT: I'll not repeat the old clichés,
but I will suggest seriously that when
you're driving, the life you save may be
your own, the life of a member of your
family or mine. Think about the grief and
the trouble that can be caused in one moment
of speed or carelessness.

MOP-UP: And, in closing, let me ask who is
the better driver. Let's hope it is you,
man or woman. Both sexes have their faults
behind the wheel, causing serious accidents.
All know the safe-driving rules. All need
to obey the common-sense laws and avoid
recklessness.

Probably, fifty years ago there were
as many reckless drivers as there are today,
but in those days they were driving something that had more sense than they had.

Speech-O-Gram 20

WELCOMING ADDRESS

Vital Togetherness

The speech which follows was presented by a school-board member before the annual convention of the American Association of School Personnel Administrators. Its purpose is to establish a pleasant working relationship between the administrators and school-board members. It is designed to entertain, instruct, and inspire.

group:_____

address:_____time:_____

title: VITAL TOGETHERNESS

Time
(min.)

SCOOP: During luncheon, Mr. Westfall mentioned your main interests at this meeting: night clubs, Jai Alai, the horses...no, no. I beg your pardon. He told me that school administrators had too many bosses, especially board members; therefore, my subject (see title). Understand, I'm a school-board member myself.

JUMP-OFF: We have an acrobatic member who can open his mouth, put his foot in it and stand on the fence, all at the same time. Objective A: George Washington could broad jump 23 feet and that was quite a record. Today, we all know board members who can side-step farther than that. Joking aside, our schools have a serious job to do. They must be placed on solid policy-making and administrative ground. Your part in the work is vital.
Objective B: My purposes today are to welcome you to Dade County (I do this with great pleasure) and to offer a few thoughts on school administration from the board member's viewpoint.

Objective C: Vital concerns will be: better
working relationships between the board and
administrators; and how together we can all
do a better job for the children.
Promise: Having considered these matters,
perhaps you will gain greater insight into
the attitude of school-board members, find
ways of working together and thus make the
operation run more smoothly.

ADVANCE: (point 1) Let us think first about
the basis for good working relationships:
improved human relations.
Story: The administrator's job is a tough
one. One school board in Indiana decided to
build a new school. After much discussion,
they passed the following resolution: "Be
it resolved that this school district shall
have constructed a new school building. In
view of the increasing cost of materials,
the new building shall be constructed of
the materials now in the existing school
building. And, be it further resolved that
to avoid interruption of school functions,
the present school building shall be continued in use until the new school is ready
for occupancy."
          Rather difficult to administer, huh?
Times like these test men's souls, and we
need patience with the other fellow. The
board members are driven by different motives than administrators. Put yourself
in their shoes, and gain understanding.

ADVANCE: (point 2) The second consideration: How together board members and administrators can do a better job for the
children.
          (Tell story about Mark Twain and a
lady caller.)

Working at odds creates confusion when everyone in the system has the same big job to do. All need to establish the same goals and agree on the procedures, so as to arrive at objectives with efficiency.

Such instruments as a clearly worded policy manual prepared by the school administrators, approved by the board, and an informal, joint bi-monthly luncheon with an informative discussion on various aspects of administration, iron out many problems.

Such efforts pay off in improved understanding and better working relationships.

ASSAULT: The story is told about the lady in our neighborhood who used to quiet her barking dog with the words, "Be quiet, Administrator, be quiet." Then, one day, a friend noticed that she said to him. "Be quiet School Board Member." The friend asked her why she called her dog by a different name and the lady replied, "Well, he used to sit and howl. Now, he just sits."

We all know that neither condition is right for the accomplishment of our important purpose. Together we must work for the good of the youth of our nation.

MOP-UP: I have used up my time and must close. As I do, let me say again that we need to strive continually for improved human relations between the board members and school administrators so that cooperatively we can do a more effective job in providing educational leadership for our public schools.

Again, let me say it is a real pleasure having you with us in Dade County and we hope your stay will be pleasant and your return prompt.

ORIENTATION TALK

Humanities' Horn of Plenty

This talk is informative and, at the same time, inspirational. It is designed to orient college students who are entering a course in the humanities. The purpose of the speech is twofold: to explain what they will study, and also what they will gain from the course. This same format can be adjusted to the orientation of any group on any subject.

Speech-O-Gram 21: ORIENTATION TALK

group:_____

address:_____time:_____

title: HUMANITIES' HORN OF PLENTY

Time
(min.)

SCOOP: Sophomores have told me that most students who sign up for the course in humanities don't know what they're getting into. I've taught the subject for several semesters, and would add that a lot of them don't know what they're flunking out of when the course is over. Therefore, I decided to talk on (see title).

JUMP-OFF: "Experience is what keeps a man who makes the same mistake twice from admitting it the third time around."
Objective A: This is a self-evident truth. Some people go from one mistake to another, never completely happy or successful. They lack the principal ingredient of success and happiness in their lives — an education. As a result, they fail. You need not fall into this category.
Objective B: Let us look at an ingredient that is lacking in the lives of people who are not fully successful — knowledge of the humanities.
Objective C: Our chief considerations will be:
       The branches of polite learning which constitute the humanities, and how a knowl-

edge of these subjects can be helpful to
you as individuals.
<u>Promise:</u> Having gained such knowledge, you
will be better qualified to cope with this
discipline and be better prepared to live
the full life. You will have made the great
cultural achievements of mankind your own.

ADVANCE: <u>(point 1)</u> First, what branches
of learning are dealt with under the heading "humanities"? They are art, music, and
literature.
<u>Story:</u> Art is the accumulation of all crea-
tive works of mankind. According to Philip
C. Beam in <u>The Language of Art,</u> "...through
art we can gain an aggregate of intellectual, emotional, and spiritual experiences
far stronger, clearer, and more sensitive
than our own." Thus, you see that such
knowledge strengthens your life. A knowledge
of painting, sculpture and architecture
through the ages intensifies your life's
experiences.
        Music deals in the same commodities,
advancing emotions and intellect. As Ulrich
has said in <u>Music: A Design for Listening,</u>
"A musical experience is first of all an
adventure in emotion; but it is also an
intellectual adventure."
        Literature — "the thought of thinking
souls" (Thomas Carlyle) — is the final
great helpmeet to the scholar who seeks
to profit from the creative works of learned
men.

ADVANCE: <u>(point 2)</u> These are the humanities, which will constitute your course.
Why is it important that you learn about
your great heritage of art, music and literature?
        Art, for example, represents the feel-

ings of the people, their government, cultural development, their religious beliefs and attitudes. And so it is with music and literature. Your study of contributions in these areas will give you a vivid picture of the lives of people from the earliest times up to the present moment, and, from this knowledge, you will gain strength in your own life.

ASSAULT: Somebody once asked Dr. Charles W. Eliot, the prominent Harvard educator, how his school had gained its prestige as the greatest storehouse of knowledge in the nation. "In all likelihood," said Dr. Eliot, "it is because the freshmen bring us so much of it, and the seniors take away so little." On the other hand, Ben Franklin said, "Knowledge is the only instrument of production that is not subject to diminishing returns." Dr. Eliot was being facetious; Ben was serious, his thinking sound. Great returns come to the student who discovers the great treasury contained in art, music and literature of all ages.

MOP-UP: In closing, let me review the areas of the humanities:

Art, which helps to interpret, clarify and intensify life's experiences; music, which advances the emotions and the intellect; and literature, which gives insight into the thinking of great men. By learning about these contributions, you will gain intellectual strength; the contributions tend to become part of you as you study them. Napoleon said, "Great men are meteors designed to burn so that the earth may be lighted." Your study of the humanities permits you to see and profit from the light cast by these great meteors.

Speech-O-Gram 22

AFTER-LUNCHEON TALK

Our Priceless Heritage

Recently, civic clubs have devoted considerable time to talks on Americanism vs. Communism and members have shown much more than a passing interest in the subject. The speech outlined here was presented at a meeting of Kiwanis and was limited to fifteen minutes, the usual amount of time allowed for after-luncheon speeches at civic club meetings. The content is persuasive and inspirational.

Speech-O-Gram 22: AFTER-LUNCHEON TALK

group:_____

address:_____time:_____

title: OUR PRICELESS HERITAGE

Time
(min.)

SCOOP: When Mr. Easley asked me to speak with you tonight, he told me of your concern over the tenable position of America in the world today. For that reason, I have decided to speak on (see title). In Rotary, as in Lions Clubs, we too have devoted time in recent meetings to Americanism.

JUMP-OFF: (Story about Mr. Einstein's comment regarding World War III.)

<u>Objective A:</u> Such a statement has obvious meaning to all of us here and is positive proof that: Communism in the world and in America is a stern reality, a way of life contrary to our heritage of freedom, our belief in God, our trust, love, good will toward all men, justice and mercy.

<u>Objective B:</u> Therefore, let us face reality squarely and try to discover how we can effectively repel this blood-red current that drowns weak nations.

<u>Objective C:</u> Vital concerns will be: The facts about Communism — facts that put the spotlight on the threat, the danger, the tactics, the tools.

184

Faith in the American way and what we must do to preserve our way of life.
Promise: Having considered these matters, you will gain new insights into this grave danger and, I hope, be inspired to become even more agressive in your stand for the American way.

ADVANCE: (point 1) First, let us look at a few facts about Communism.
Story: Patrick Henry said courageously: "Give me liberty or give me death." Recently, I have heard a few mealymouths say, "I'd rather be Red than dead." This alarms me — what kind of American thinking is this?

J. Edgar Hoover in Masters of Deceit (Henry Holt, N.Y., 1958) says Communism "would strip man of his belief in God, his heritage of freedom, his trust in love, justice and mercy. Under Communism, all would become, as so many already have, twentieth-century slaves." The intent of the Communists is to rule the world. Their tools include scare tactics, and the principles of divide and conquer, infiltration, destruction of faith, lies. We've seen these working in Berlin and Laos, Czechoslovakia, Rumania, Bulgaria, Hungary and Poland.

America loves peace, but not the peace of a cemetery.

ADVANCE: (point 2) Therefore, let us next consider what we can personally do to help hold back the flow of the Red tide. We can work hard for freedom, tirelessly, intelligently, with personal sacrifices of time and money. The Communists have given up much for their cause, which is enslavement of the

world. Certainly, freedom for the peoples of
the world is worth any personal sacrifice.
We must work to strengthen democratic institutions — the church, home, school, government. Know the facts and be able to recognize
the insidious and subtle manner in which
Communism infiltrates the nation. Rekindle
American faith, based on our priceless heritage of freedom, justice and religious
spirit. Express our pride in our traditions
and ideals. As parents, protect and guide
the children; as teachers, preserve the
classrom from Communism.

ASSAULT: Most of all, we must work for unity
of purpose — stand together, work together
as free men, proud of the great Christian
heritage that our fathers and their fathers
fought so ably to preserve.
        Cling tenaciously to Christian ideals
and practices. Today, more than ever before,
we need faith — strong, genuine faith. We
need to flex Christian muscles and to move
offensively forward.

MOP-UP: Let me remind you before I close:
Communism is a real threat to America. The
atheistic Red leaders fully intend to place
free peoples in slavery, stamp out Christianity, the home, government by the people
and every vestige of democracy. As free men,
we can oppose them. We must stand firm in
our Christian faith and as American citizens: Work for freedom; know the facts about
Communism; strengthen our democratic institutions; rekindle the American spirit;
protect and guide our children; work for
unity of purpose; and cling to Christian
ideals.

Speech-O-Gram 23

APPEAL FOR CHARITABLE SERVICES

The Kid in Ward 5

An appeal for funds, old clothes, services, or blood donations develops easily when it is organized with a Speech-O-Gram. With the story of "The Kid in Ward 5" in the Jump-off, the attention of the audience is caught immediately, and after that the speaker encounters little resistance as he makes his appeal.

Speech-O-Gram 23: APPEAL FOR CHARITABLE SERVICES

group:_____

address:_____time:_____

title: THE KID IN WARD 5

Time
(min.)

SCOOP: Your chairman has outlined the excellent work you have been doing for crippled children and your other activities in behalf of youth. I was happy to hear of this because your benevolent interest come so close to my topic: (see title). His was a specific case, but it could happen to any child.

JUMP-OFF: The Kid was in trouble. He needed help...fast! He was bleeding to death, etc.
Objective A: An experience such as this proves that all of us need to "Play ball," and to recognize the values of having a supply of blood readily available in the bank. We need to see how easy it is to make the contribution which may some day save the life of another human being.
Objective B: My purpose is to show the values of such giving, so that each of you will gladly leave your donation at the Blood Bank this week.
Objective C: First, we will consider the mechanics of how go about giving blood; and second, why we need to make this worthwhile community effort.

188

<u>Promise</u>: If you respond as I know you will, you will gain credit for yourself and your club. You will know that you have done something to save the life of another person.

ADVANCE: <u>(point 1)</u> First, let us talk about the mechanics of donating blood.
<u>Story</u>: It's really very simple — no need for a problem like the one the night nurse got into when she plugged her patient's electric blanket into the automatic toaster. Next morning, the old gentleman told his doctor about it. "I didn't mind too much, but every four minutes it popped me out of bed."

The Blood Bank works a lot better than that. At the beginning, several people donated blood so that all types would be available. Now, everyone can use the blood, but must pledge to repay the bank with a similar quantity. Anyone can borrow, but someone must put it back.

All you need do is to go to a Red Cross Blood Donor Station and tell them you wish to give blood. It takes only a few minutes and only one thing hurts: you must not eat for four hours before you give blood. Your club can have credit and you get a record of your gift. It's as easy as that.

ADVANCE: <u>(point 2)</u> Now, look at the values: You and your club have credit in the Blood Bank and your deposit yields high interest in many forms.

It gives assurance and security just as any bank account does. Without it, the story of the Kid in Ward 5 might not have had such a happy ending.

Even though we may never have to use our "money in the bank" we can feel the comfort and satisfaction that comes from knowing that we have played a part — no small part — in helping another stay healthy and alive.

ASSAULT: Story of the famous cartoonist who decided to send twenty of his friends a one-word telegram: "Congratulations."

Your participation as a blood donor may be simple from a time-and-trouble standpoint, but it will be no minor achievement for you or your club. It is vitally important that you do this: We want and need more assets in the Blood Bank so that we will be able to cope with the problem of the Kid in Ward 5 and with any other emergency, whether it involves your wife, your children, you, or anyone else.

MOP-UP: The mechanics are simple and the values are immeasurable in human lives and suffering.

The Kid in Ward 5 might be merely a statistic today had it not been for people like yourselves who were willing to take a few minutes of their time to give to the Blood Bank.

Don't delay. Get over to your Red Cross Blood Donor Station today. The address is Fifth Street at Pine Avenue.

Speech-O-Gram 24

INTRODUCTION (FORMAL)

Dr. Edward Robinson Squibb
Physician, Pharmacist, Chemist

If the reader were to step back into history a few years (circa 1870) he might find himself presiding at a meeting where Dr. Edward Robinson Squibb would be the main speaker. Under these circumstances, with a group of physicians or nurses as his audience, his Speech-O-Gram for a brief introductory talk could be formulated as shown. For the most part, this presentation is informative and neither slights nor exaggerates the speaker's background and qualifications as a speaker. However, it does build up his importance and sets the stage for his presentation.

group:_____

address:_____time:_____

title: DR. EDWARD ROBINSON SQUIBB
Physician, Pharmacist, Chemist

Time
(min.)

SCOOP: Ladies and gentlemen, our president suggested that we should have a report on the pure food and drug laws of our state and asked me to find a qualified speaker. I followed up on his idea and had the good fortune of obtaining (see title) who wrote the laws.

JUMP-OFF: The subject of his talk brings to mind the story of the parson and the devout old Negress.
Objective A: The pure food and drug laws are meant to protect everyone — especially those of us in the medical profession. Therefore, it is important that we become closely acquainted with the new standards so that we may be more alert for infractions.
Objective B: Let us learn all we can from Dr. Squibb, who has consented to answer questions at the end of his talk.
Objective C: In my all-too-brief introduction, I want to give you a few general facts

192

about our speaker and list some of his epoch-
making accomplishments.

Promise: An acquaintance with the man and
his firsthand review of the laws will help
all of us to gain a better insight into the
purposes and far-reaching effects of this
legislation.

ADVANCE: (point 1) First, let us find out
something about the man himself.

Story: Dr. Squibb was born in Wilmington,
Del., in 1819. He received his M.D. degree
at Jefferson Medical College, Philadelphia,
in 1845, and practiced medicine in Philadelphia for two years. He joined the U. S.
Navy as assistant surgeon in 1847 and served
at sea for four years. Afterwards, he was
assigned to duty at the naval hospital in
Brooklyn, N. Y., where he began his career
as a manufacturing pharmacist and chemist.
He opened civilian laboratories in Brooklyn,
in 1858.

ADVANCE: (point 2) As to his significant
accomplishments, to name just a few, while
in the Navy he proposed making basic phar-
maceuticals to replace inferior shipboard
drugs. He was the first to distill ether
with steam. Through professional societies
and revision committees of the United States
Pharmacopoeia, he waged constant war on
quacks, nostrums and adulteration.

As many of you know, Dr. Squibb re-
covered from severe burns suffered when
ether exploded at his chemical and pharma-
ceutical laboratory in Brooklyn. While he
was recovering, he made plans for the new
laboratory which he operates at the present
time.

ASSAULT: Dr. Squibb is a man of unswerving integrity and fearless determination. These attributes coupled with his tremendous learning and skill have won for him a place of high position in his profession and in the hearts of all who have had the opportunity to come to know him personally and through his good work.

MOP-UP: I count it a rare privilege to introduce to you tonight a man of inventive genius, who has contributed so much to the welfare of mankind in general, and specifically to the people of New York and New Jersey, through the formulation of the pure food and drug laws for these two states. Now, it is my great honor to present Dr. Edward Robinson Squibb.

ADDRESS TO YOUTH GROUP

Roads to Success in College

When addressing a group of young people, the speaker who limits his talk to a few minutes and at the same time puts some spice in it, makes himself popular with his audience. Although the occasion may be quite formal, some humor is desirable because of the age and interests of the listeners. The speech can be inspirational because, surprisingly enough, that's the way the audience likes it.

Speech-O-Gram 25: ADDRESS TO YOUTH GROUP

group:_____

address:_____time:_____

title: ROADS TO SUCCESS IN COLLEGE

Time
(min.)

SCOOP: Your principal has told me that academically and in many other ways this is an outstanding class and that many of you plan to go on to college. Others are wavering between college and a job. I was happy to learn of your interests because they come so close to my own subject for tonight (see title).

JUMP-OFF: An old Dutch proverb tells us: "God has given the birds their food, but He does not throw it in the nest."
Objective A: This is a good formula for all of you, regardless of your plans. In life, there are precious opportunities all about us. We must have the urge and the initiative if we are to take advantage of them. The trouble with most people is they itch for what they want, but they won't scratch for it.
Objective B: My purpose tonight is to help you to realize that to reach a college degree you will have to stand on tiptoe. At the same time, I want to encourage your very best efforts.

196

Objective C: My principal consideration
will be your urge to learn, and your will
to become an educated man or woman.
Promise: If you will remember these few
points, I'm certain your years in college
will be a rich and satisfying experience.

ADVANCE: (point 1) Let us consider the
motivation without which any prospective
student is doomed to failure in the college
or university - the urge to become educated.
Story: Some young people are like my little
girl who closed her prayer one night with:
"And Lord, please start putting the vita-
mins I need in ice cream instead of in
lettuce and spinach."
        The trouble is that we look no farther
ahead than Saturday night. We want only the
goodies. Urges often run in wrong directions—a new car, a motorcycle, a temporary
toy. There's time for these later, but the
time for a sound education is now, while
you're young. You need to think in terms of
long-range accomplishments. I know I can
perk up your enthusiasm for college with
a statisical finding: namely, that your
high-school diploma is worth $49,000 in
future earnings. Each year of college adds
$25,000.
        Accomplishments result from work;
dreaming gets nothing done. Even if you're
on the right track, you'll be run over if
you just sit there and dream.

ADVANCE: (point 2) Next, consider the key
with which almost any normal person can
unlock the door to success in college — the
will to become an educated man or woman.
        Ty Cobb had one burning ambition — to

be always first. He set out to make good, and
did. George M. Cohan, playwright, song writer,
director, actor, dancer, producer, was all
that for half a century. He was the hardest
worker the theatre ever had, and his success
was great. Rocky Marciano, the fighter, had
one burning ambition: to be undefeatd heavy-
weight champion of the world. He worked, sac-
rificed, gave up all pleasures; finally, he
made it.

You can succeed in college if you have
the same kind of drive and determination.

ASSAULT: I like an expression I heard just
recently: "The difficult we do immediately;
the impossible takes a little longer."

I'm sure that's the way it was with Cobb,
Cohan, Marciano, and most of the greats in
any game. And you can do as well. You won't,
though, if they say of you, "All he does is
go out for coffee breaks"; "That girl is on
dead center"; "He is willing to do anything
once, with the possible exception of work";
"She needs a birth certificate to prove she
was born."

MOP-UP: Seriously, as I bring my remarks to
a close, let me urge all of you to decide in
favor of the long-range objectives of higher
education. Be willing to give up the temporary
pleasures, so that you gain greater strength
through study and increased learning. Let it
be said of you that he (or she) stays at the
job of becoming an educated man (or woman)
like an hourglass pouring out its sand.

My sand has run out...good luck!

III QUOTES AND ANECDOTES

ACHIEVEMENT

They are able because they think they are able.

Vergil—*Aeneid*

He that is overcautious will accomplish little.

Johann von Schiller—*Wilhelm Tell*

Get good counsel before you begin and when you have decided, act promptly.

Sallust—*Catilina*

A conference is a gathering of important people who singly can do nothing, but together can decide that nothing can be done.

Fred Allen

We can walk a hundred miles easily if we walk each mile with a firm, steady step.

It is necessary to try to surpass one's self always this occupation ought to last as long as life.

Queen Christina

Slumber not in the tents of your fathers. The world is advancing. Advance with it.

Giuseppe Mazzini

ADVICE

One February night, Rusty Pipes, the plumber, was awakened by the jangle of his telephone.

"Hello, this is Dr. Boyles. My basement is flooding. Can you come right over and fix it?"

"You expect me to get dressed and come over to your house in the middle of the night? You must think I'm some kind of a nut."

"Listen, lots of people call me in the middle of the night, when they're in trouble."

"Yeah, right! What seems to be the matter with your plumbing?"

"Stopped up I guess."

"Okeh . . . drop a pink pill down the drain and if everything ain't all right in the morning I'll make a house call."

Never give advice in a crowd.

Arab Proverb

A man should first direct himself in the way he should go. Only then should he instruct others.

Buddha

AMBITION

Ask, and it shall be given you; seek, and ye shall find; knock, and it shall be opened unto you.

Matthew 7:7

Too many people itch for what they want, but won't scratch for it.

Even if you are on the right track, you will be run over if you just sit there.

Ambition has one trait, I find—
It never stops to look behind.

Richard Maxwell

The only thing worse than being in a rut is having no road at all.

AMERICANA

Give me your tired, your poor . . .
I lift my lamp beside the golden door.
> Emma Lazarus—"The New Colossus:
> Inscription for the
> Statue of Liberty"

Two tourists were discussing certain parts of the West.

Mike (the Finger) said, "Take Arizona . . . without Reno and Las Vegas, what yuh got left?"

Knuckles McGoon thought about it for awhile and finally replied, "Well . . . ah . . . yuh got the Grand Canyon."

I come from a state that raises corn and cotton and cockleburs and Democrats, and frothy eloquence neither convinces nor satisfies me. I am from Missouri. You have got to show me.
> William D. Vandiver—Speech, 1899

P. T. Barnum, the great showman, once received a letter from a Vermonter offering him a cherry-colored cat for $600. Always on the lookout for a novelty for his show, Barnum sent the $600— after getting the man's solemn word that the creature was cherry colored. A crate arrived. Barnum opened it and a black cat jumped out. Around its neck was a ribbon and from the ribbon hung a note which read:

"Up in Vermont our cherries are black."

An American tourist refused to be too greatly impressed with the masterpieces at the Louvre. "We've got plenty of priceless canvases in the U.S. too," he declared.

"I know," said his guide. "Rembrandt painted seven hundred pictures in his lifetime, and America has all ten thousand of them."

One day in school, the teacher asked Chester who signed the Declaration of Independence.

"I don't know," said the boy, "and I don't give a damn."

The teacher called in the father and told him what his son had said.

"Now, Chester," the man drawled, "if you signed that Declaration, come out and admit it."

ANIMALS

The spade cut the fishworms in two. Said the worm, "From now on I'll be living a double life."

I feel like a frog in the middle of an eight-lane highway with her hopper busted.

An owl married a goat and they had a very happy life together until their child was born. Turned out to be a Hootinanny.

A man was driving his panel truck down the road with his right hand on the wheel and the other out of the cab, holding a baseball bat. Every now and then he would reach back and slam the bat up against the back end of the truck.

Two policemen who were parked behind a billboard noticed the action, chased him down, and asked him to explain.

"Well, it's like this," he said seriously, "this is a two-ton truck. I got a load of three tons of parakeets in there and I have to keep one-third of 'em flying all the time."

APPEARANCE

God has given you one face, and you make yourselves another.
William Shakespeare—*Hamlet*

She had nothing on, but the radio.

A barber said to his customer, "Young man, your hair is getting thin."
"Okeh, okeh," said the customer. "Who wants fat hair?"

I have a new suit . . . got it at Sears. It's a Sears' sucker.

Two soldiers were on a transport going overseas. Standing on the deck they gazed out across the vast expanse of water.
"That's the most water I ever seen in my whole life," said one. "Did you ever see so much water?"
His companion said, "You ain't seen nothing yet. That's just the top of it."

From a distance it is something; and nearby it is nothing.
                                        Jean de La Fontaine

A group of men were discussing Stephen Douglas and his physical peculiarities. Abraham Lincoln happened to join them at this point and, turning from the specific subject under discussion, one of them asked the President how long he thought a man's legs should be.
"Well," drawled Lincoln, "I should think a man's legs ought to reach from his body to the ground."

AVERAGE MAN

The average man knows as much about an atomic bomb as he does about his income tax form.

Public opinion, though often formed upon a wrong basis, yet generally has a strong underlying sense of justice.
                                        Abraham Lincoln

Most of us look no further ahead than next Saturday night.

BEATNIK JOKES

A Beatnik walked down Bourbon Street in New Orleans snapping his fingers. Another Beat stopped him and asked why he was snapping his fingers like that.

"That's to keep the elephants away."

"Man, you're crazy, there ain't an elephant within miles."

"You see, it works."

A hepcat died and on his tombstone were the words, "Don't dig me now, I'm really gone."

A Beatnik was walking down Madison Avenue when he met a fellow Beatnik. "Hey, man," he said, "how do I get to Carnegie Hall?"

The other Beatnik stod snapping his fingers for a few moments, then said, "Practice, man, practice."

Yeah, that's the way the Mercedes Benz.

BUSINESS

The president of a dog-food company called a meeting of all his salesmen and at the start of the meeting asked, "Who has the best dog food?"

He pointed at one of his employees and the man said emphatically, "We have."

He pointed at another and the answer was the same.

After getting a convincing "Ours," from several of the men, he asked, "Well, if ours is the best, why is it not selling?"

All was quiet for a long time. Then, finally, a little fellow in the back row held up his hand, "I can tell you why it is not selling. The dogs won't eat it."

A clothing merchant on Lincoln Road in Miami Beach was asked about the mark-up on his merchandise.

"I buy sometimes for one dollar," he explained. "I sell it for four dollars . . . three per cent mark-up, that ain't bad."

A merchant was on his deathbed and in his last few moments asked, in a heavy breath,

"Is Mamma here?"

"Yes, Mamma is here, Father," came the reply from the eldest son.

"Is Rosie here?"

"Yes, Rosie is here, Father."

"Is Abie here?"

"Yes, Abie is here, Father."

"Is Rubin here?"

"Yes, Rubin is here."

"Well, then," yelled the old gentleman, "who's out watching the store?"

CHARACTER

Character is the soundest happiness.

> Richard Maxwell

Never throw mud. You may miss your mark, but you must have dirty hands.

> Joseph Parker

Strength grows stronger by being tried.

> Seneca—*Ad Lucilium*

Good humor is goodness and wisdom combined.

> Owen Meredith

As unconquerable as chewing gum.

Give a fellow an inch and he thinks he's a ruler.

We dismiss a boy's antics with the comment, "Boys will be boys"—but we must remember that boys will be men one day.

People seldom improve when they have no other model but themselves to copy after.

Oliver Goldsmith

CHILDREN

When thou wast young, thou girdedst thyself, and walkedst wither thou wouldest: but when thou shalt be old, thou shalt stretch forth thy hands, and another shall gird thee, and carry thee whither thou wouldest not.

John 21:18

A high school teacher asked Phillip to name a time saver. The boy thought for a moment and then replied, "Love at first sight."

In the modern home, everything is controlled by switches except the children.

At bedtime recently, the father told Mary to put out the cat. The daughter replied, "I didn't know it was on fire."

Our daughter's definition of kisses: "Little patches of wet stuff."

The little boy came home from school. His mother asked him why he was crying.
"One of the kids at school called me a sissy."
"What did you do?" he mother asked.
"I hit him with my purse."

The teacher took her class to the zoo and they moved from cage to cage learning about the animals. Finally they got to the cage where the deer was.

"Now, children, you know what this is," said the teacher. "It's what your mother calls your daddy when he comes home after working all day."

They all looked at the deer for awhile and finally little Fletcher down in the front row wrinkled up his nose, looked up at the teacher and said, "You mean to tell me a louse is that big?"

At home, Johnny asked his parents where he came from.
"The stork brought you," his mother told him.
"What about you and Daddy?"
"The stork brought us too."
"Well what about Grandma and Grandpa?"
"The stork brought them, also."
The next day in school, the teacher asked Johnny to tell about his birth. The little eight-year-old scratched his head. "I don't know. In our family, there hasn't been a natural birth in years."

CLERGY

A preacher was invited into a neighboring county to a picnic. Expecting to say the blessing or give the invocation, he asked the chairman what he wanted him to do.

"We'd like to have you do some hog calling."

The minister, a little hurt, thought for a minute, then said, "Over where I come from, they look on me as Shepherd of the Sheep, but then you know your people."

A preacher took part in a home-town play and the script called for the line, "My God, I'm shot!"

The man of the cloth objected to the wording so the director changed it to, "My goodness, I'm shot."

On the night of the play, some catsup was thrown onto the

preacher's shirt just before he uttered his line. He didn't notice it at first and went ahead, "My goodness, I'm shot."

As he started to fall to the floor, he saw the red splotch for the first time.

"My God," he yelled, "I *am* shot!"

A brilliant priest, Father Sicola, served his job faithfully for several years but was never promoted. One day he said to the cardinal, "Why is it I have not been promoted?" The cardinal said, "We have thought about it many times, Joe. We realize that you could go all the way to the top but how would it look in the papers if we had a Pope Sicola?"

The test of a preacher is that his congregation goes away saying not, "What a lovely sermon," but, "I will do something."

St. Francis de Sales

From Europe comes the story of the village priest who told his congregation: "Next Sunday I will give a sermon about liars. I want you all to read Chapter 17 of St. Mark."

On Sunday the priest said: "Those who read Chapter 17 of St. Mark raise their hands."

Almost all the hands went up. Then he explained: "St. Mark has only sixteen chapters. I will now give a sermon about liars."

CONSCIENCE

We must regard ourselves not as owners, but as trustees of our wealth.

A man rushed into the stationer's store and asked the clerk, "Got a 'No vacancy' sign?"

"Yeh, I can fix you up, Joe. Your apartment building all filled up?"

"No, it's for my fall-out shelter."

A New England conscience doesn't keep you from doing things; it just keeps you from enjoying things you do.

God and conscience are on the same side—always.

DETERMINATION

The great pleasure in life is doing what people say you cannot do.
Walter Bagehot—*Literary Studies*

The strongest of the human instincts is the impulse to sit down.

A traveling man caught in a torrential rainstorm stopped at a farmhouse overnight. Next morning he looked out on the flood and watched pieces of fence, chicken coops, branches, and an old straw hat float past with the current. Then he saw the straw hat come back past the house. Then he saw it go down again. He wondered if he'd gone mad.

Finally, he called the landlady and pointed to the hat. "Oh," she said, after a glance out the window, "that must be Grandpa. He said yesterday that in spite of fire, hades, or high water he was going to mow the yard today."

Firmness—That admirable quality in ourselves which is detestable stubbornness in others.

A young boy entered the bank and walked up to the first window, shoved a five-dollar bill onto the counter and asked for change. He stood back and carefully counted it and moved to the next window.

"Will you please change this for a five-dollar bill?" he asked the teller.

He continued this procedure down the long line of cages, with a vice president looking on. When he neared the last window, the bank official walked up and asked why he was bothering clerks in this manner.

The boy looked up at the man and said, "I figure someone is going to make a mistake and it won't be me."

DRUNKS

A drunk got confused and started driving down a one-way street in the wrong direction. A cop saw him and blew his whistle.

"Hey," he yelled, "couldn't you see those arrows back there?"

"Sure didn't . . . I didn't even see the Indians."

A gravedigger dug so deep he couldn't get out. He yelled for help and a drunk came along.

"Get me out of here," the man pleaded. "I'm cold."

"No wonder you're cold," said the drunk, "you don't have any dirt on you."

"Not only do I have all these troubles," the lady told the bartender, "but I've got heartburn."

"Lady, you don't have heartburn," the barkeep replied. "You're leaning too close to that ashtray."

A drunk got out of his car, staggered to the parking meter, put in a nickel and the pointer moved over to sixty.

The drunk looked at it alarmed and said, "Geez—I've lost 100 lbs."

A drunk said to the taxi driver, "Do you know where the Alcoholics Anonymous is?"

"You want to join?" the driver asked.

"Nope," hiccupped the drunk, "I wanna resign."

A man who had imbibed too heavily at a party staggered toward his car. A woman who was looking on watched his efforts and said,

"You're not going to drive home in that condition I hope?"
"I have to drive," he said, "I'm too drunk to walk."

Two drunks were walking down a railroad track. Finally, after some struggle, the first drunk said, "I wouldn't mind this so much if these steps weren't so steep."

They plodded on a little longer and finally the second drunk said, "I don't mind that so much, it's just that these handrails are so low."

An Irishman was making a confession when the priest said, "Mr. O'Leary, it appears you've been drinking heavily."
"Just a wee nip of Three Fathers, Feather."

EDUCATION

There are five tests of the evidence of education—correctness and precision in use of the mother tongue; refined and gentle manners, the result of fixed habits of thought and action; sound standards of appreciation of beauty and of worth, and a character based on those standards; power and habit of reflection; efficiency of the power to do.

Nicholas Murray Butler

A small college in Georgia was looking for a new president and they had sent a member of their board of trustees to a Georgia university in search of candidates. The board member told the president, "Now, we don't want anyone lower than a dean."
"That ought to be easy," replied the president, "there's no one lower than a dean."

A great financier once said: "I go to school every time I meet a person. I never lose the opportunity to get a man's point of view, no matter who he is."

If a person has no education he just has to use his brains.

A class in education: A bunch of squares in a circle.

Reading maketh a full man; conference a ready man; and writing an exact man.

                                        Francis Bacon—*Essays*

Grandpa had been busy in the parlor all evening. Finally, Grandma yelled, "What are you doing, Silas?"

"I just learned to write, Sarah," the old gentleman replied.

"Land of goodness," she exclaimed, "what does it say?"

"Don't know," said Silas. "I ain't larned to read yet."

This fellow has so many degrees he's known as "the human thermometer."

A professor at Indiana University asked a young lady in his class the question, "If you were to divide all the people in America into four distinct groups, what would they be?"

She thought about the question a moment and replied, "Actives, pledges, rushees and alumni."

The principal of a high school was talking to a school board member about his many duties.

"I suppose you get many invitations to give speeches in the community," the school board member said.

"Yes, yes, I sure do," said the educator, "but I have to tell them I don't want to get too far from my school because that's where I earn my bread and oleo."

John is a fine, educated fellow. He studied agriculture at Arkansas State and when he graduated, his classmates voted him "the most likely to sack seed."

ENTHUSIASM

Nothing great was ever achieved without enthusiasm.
Ralph Waldo Emerson—*On Circles*

The world belongs to the Enthusiast who keeps cool.
William McFee—*Casuals of the Sea*

Zeal: The enthusiasm with which we point out another's mistakes.

An idea, to be suggestive, must come to the individual with the force of a revelation.
William James—*The Varieties of*
Religious Experience

EXCELLENCE

Trifles make perfection, but perfection is no trifle.
Michelangelo

Excellent things are rare.
Plato—*The Republic*

Nature has made two kinds of excellent minds: the one to produce beautiful thoughts and beautiful actions, the other to admire them.
Joseph Joubert

EXPERIENCE

Some learn from experience. Others never recover from it.

After the city boy, who was visiting a farm, had milked his first cow, the farmer said, "Well, you learned something new today."

The city boy replied, "Yes, I learned that the man who says a cow gives milk is a liar."

I have but one lamp by which my feet are guided, and that is the lamp of experience.

Patrick Henry

FAITH

I have never known a thinking man who did not believe in God.

Robert A. Millikan, scientist,
Nobel Prize winner

Faith is nothing but a living wide-awake consciousness of the God within.

The Good Lord gave you the dark to sleep by and the light to eat by.

Honor from God is the important thing—not from men.

Never in my life have I made an important decision without Divine guidance.

Henry Ford

A Protestant boy wanted to marry a Catholic girl. She insisted that he go into her church. He did so. A few weeks later a friend asked the girl if John had gone into the church. The girl put her hand to her face and wept, "Yes, and now he wants to become a priest."

FEAR

When afraid, stop and think. Examine the feared situation. See if there is any real danger in it. If not, try just that act to which the fear is attached.

John Dollard

Ignorance is the mother of fear.

Henry Home

Often the test of courage is not to die but to live.

Vittorio Alfieri—*Orestes*

Nothing stands between you and your highest ideals—between you and every desire of your heart—but doubt and fear.

FOOD

Show me a twelve-year-old boy who gets to order his own breakfast in a restaurant and I'll show you a kid with a chocolate malted milk.

The Irishman told his friend, "I don't like spinach and I'm glad I don't like spinach because if I liked spinach I'd eat spinach and I hate the durned stuff."

I've got a frog in my throat—first solid food I've had all day.

Bob Hope

Husbands these days want their wives to bake bread the way their mothers did.

On the other hand, the wives want their husbands to make dough like their fathers did.

I am about people as I am about foods. I know which of them gives me indigestion.

GOALS

Decide what your goal will be; consider whether it is right that you do this; and, if it is, do it . . . a little every day till done.

Sometimes you will have to prove to others that you can accomplish certain aims, but more often you must prove to *yourself* that you can do it. So doing gives you strength to go on to more important matters.

What did I do today to bring me closer to what I eventually want in life? Ask yourself that question every night.

You must have long-range goals to keep you from being frustrated by short-range failures.

Charles C. Noble

Whatsoever thy hand findeth to do, do it with thy might.

Ecclesiastes 9:10

You must keep your goal in sight,
Labor toward it day and night . . .

Witter Brynner

GOVERNMENT

A farmer had so many dandelions in his fields he didn't know what to do about them. He wrote to the Department of Agriculture for advice. Finally, he received a four-page single-spaced letter in response. In a brief, final paragraph the Washington expert said, "We really don't know. Suggest you learn to live with them."

An Alabama farmer was sitting on his front porch when the member of a survey team came up:

"Sir," said the stranger, "are you in favor of integration?"

"No," replied the farmer.

"Are you in favor of segregation?"

"No," said the Southerner.

"You ought to make up your mind about this thing," the survey man said. "If you don't believe in integration or segregation, what do you believe in?"

"I done made up my mind," the old man shrugged, "I'm for slavery."

I believe in extending foreign aid to Monaco. Everybody else gets it—why play favorites. And there's a need for another casino over there.

The young fellow said to his dad: "Dad, why do they have a chaplain in Congress?"

The father said, "They have a chaplain there to pray."

"Well, who does he pray for? Does he pray for the Congress?"

Dad replied, "Oh, no, he stands up and takes a look at the Congress, and then prays for the country!"

> Hon. Charles A. Halleck,
> member of House of Representatives
> from Indiana

HONESTY

Shawn O'Shaunessey and a friend were looking at tombstones in an old cemetery. They came to one which read: "Here lies John Jones, Attorney, and an honest man."

Shawn turned to his friend and said, "There must be two men in there."

An excuse is worse and more terrible than a lie; for an excuse is a lie guarded.

Alexander Pope

Unfaithfulness in the keeping of an appointment is an act of clear dishonesty. You may as well borrow a person's money as his time.

Horace Mann

Affectation is the product of falsehood.

Thomas Carlyle

When I was a boy of twelve, I worked at an ice-cream parlor in Elkhart, Indiana. One evening I was carrying a bag of chocolates home to my mother. I decided to stop at a restaurant and have a hot dog. When I walked out of the place I carelessly left my mother's present on the seat of the booth.

Three blocks later, I suddenly remembered. I turned and rushed back to the restaurant to get the package. I looked in the booth where I had been sitting, but they weren't there. I asked the fellow behind the counter if he'd seen the bag of chocolates.

"N . . . no, I ain't seen no chocolates," he said, fishy-eyed. Then he turned to the fellow who stood washing dishes. "You seen any bag of chocolates around here, Harry?"

"No," he grinned like the cat that had just swallowed the goldfish, "not me." Then he busied himself with the dishes.

I looked in back of the counter. There lay the empty sack, crumpled into a small ball.

"Some other customer must have carried them off," the first man said.

"Gee! That's too bad," I said. "I hope no one eats them; they're filled with rat poison."

C.R.V.D.

IGNORANCE

Fear always springs from ignorance.
                    Emerson—*The American Scholar*

Prejudice is the child of ignorance.
                                William Hazlitt

Suggested remedy for fathead: mix up a Metrecal shampoo, rub in well.

INTRODUCTIONS

I was introduced at an affair over on Cocoa Beach at a meeting of a women's club. The lady who made the introduction did an excellent job. She was most complimentary.

When she finished, I told the ladies that I didn't know when I'd had a finer introduction, except the time the person who was supposed to introduce me failed to arrive and I had to do it myself.
                    Dr. J. Bruce Wilson
                    President, Brevard Junior College

The master of ceremonies at an important banquet in New York City became flustered and said in all seriousness, "I'm about to introduce the virgin of Governor's Island."

Recently at a meeting of Rotary in the Los Angeles area, the program chairman gave a long-winded and flattering introduction of the guest speaker. When the man rose to speak, he said, "My audience does not agree with a word you say, but I will defend to the death your right to say it."

A German mayor in a small Wisconsin town had been called upon to introduce Senator Spooner. His introduction provides a pattern which all of us might follow with pleasing results: "Mine frents," said the mayor, "I haf been asked to introduce Senator Spooner, who is to make a speech. Vell, I haf did so, and he vill now do so."

KINDNESS

I expect to pass through this world but once. Any good thing, therefore, that I can do, or any kindness that I can show to any fellow creature, let me do it now. Let me not defer or neglect it, for I shall not pass this way again.

Stephen Grillet

A lady looked at her pregnant friend and said, "Are you going to have another baby?"
"No," the woman replied, "I'm carrying this one for a friend."

Kindness is the golden chain by which society is bound together.

Johann von Goethe

KNOWLEDGE

That there should one man die ignorant who had the capacity for knowledge, this I call a tragedy.

Thomas Carlyle

Frederick the Great: "The greatest and noblest pleasure which man can have in this world is to discover new truths; and the next is to shake off old prejudices."

Knowledge is of two kinds. We know a subject ourselves, or we know where we can find information upon it.

Samuel Johnson—Boswell's
Life of Johnson

Better know nothing than half-know many things.
Friedrich Nietzsche—*Thus Spake Zarathustra*

Shall I tell you what knowledge is? It is to know both what one knows and what one does not know.

Confucius

Wear your learning like your watch, in a private pocket; and do not pull it out and strike it, merely to show that you have one.
Earl of Chesterfield

Opinions founded on prejudice are always sustained with the greatest violence.

Francis Jeffrey

LISTENING

Some plague the people with too long sermons; for the faculty of listening is a tender thing, and soon becomes weary and satiated.

Martin Luther

He that hath ears to hear, let him hear.

Mark 4:9

My thoughts ran a-wool-gathering.
Miguel de Cervantes—*Don Quixote*

Hear much; speak little.

Bias

"Each of us here today has a task," said the speaker at a father and son banquet. "My task is to talk and yours to listen. And remember, I'm supposed to get finished with my task before you do yours."

Be swift to hear, slow to speak, slow to wrath.

James 1:19

Miss not the discourse of the elders.

Ecclesiasticus 8:9

Nobody ever listened himself out of a job.

Calvin Coolidge

MANNERS

Good manners is the art of making those people easy with whom we converse. Whoever makes the fewest persons uneasy, is the best bred in the company.

Jonathan Swift

Departure should be sudden.

Benjamin Disraeli

The foolish and wicked practice of profane cursing and swearing is a vice so mean and low that every person of sense and character detests and despises it.

George Washington

Politeness is the chief sign of culture.

Baltasar Gracian

No sensible person ever made an apology.

Ralph Waldo Emerson

The man ran out his front door, turned and yelled, "I don't care what your name is, get those reindeer off my roof."

MARRIAGE

I've lived a very happy life since I've been married. Just think, when I go home at night, my wife has my paper, slippers and robe waiting. She prepares a delightful dinner and afterwards, pours my hot water.

She knows how much I hate to wash dishes in cold water.

At the close of the divorce trial, the judge told the ex-husband, "I'm going to give her $50 a month alimony."

The husband brightened up, "That's great, judge. I'll throw in a few dollars every once in awhile myself."

At 2:30 A.M. in a Chicago bar a man asked his new acquaintance,

"What excuse are you going to use with your wife when you get home?"

"None," the man said.

"You mean you don't have to make excuses?"

"No, I'm just not married."

"Well, if you don't have a wife," the married man said, "why do you stay out so late?"

A man took his boss home to show him his new house. They went from room to room and finally came to the bedroom and walked through. There they saw the host's wife in the arms of another man. They walked on through without comment and into the kitchen.

"How about some coffee?" the man asked his guest.

"Yes," said the boss, "but what about that guy in the bedroom holding your wife?"

"Forget it," said the man, "let him fix his own coffee."

Bachelor: A man with no buttons on his shirts and no hand in his pockets.

My wife really knows her way around the kitchen. Now if she'd just find her way inside.

A friend of mine had his house painted last week. He was so pleased that he handed the painter an extra ten-dollar bill when he paid for the job.

"Here," he said, "take the missus out for dinner."

That evening at seven, the doorbell rang and my friend answered the door. The painter was standing there.

"What is it you want?" the man asked.

The painter, who was all dressed up now, replied, "I've come for the missus."

The newlyweds were honeymooning at the seashore. As they walked arm in arm along the beach, the young groom looked poetically out to sea and eloquently cried out: "Roll on, thou deep and dark blue ocean—roll!"

His bride gazed at the water a moment, then in hushed tones gasped, "Oh, Fred, you wonderful man! It's doing it!"

The mother of a large family announced that every Saturday there would be a prize given for the most obedient member of the family. Almost in one voice the children protested, "Oh, that isn't fair. Daddy will win every time."

OPPOSITION

An adversary may say of you that you are weak opposition—then is the time to prove that you are not.

Challenges of all sorts come along. Don't shy away. Meet them. Conquer them.

A man checked in at a small hotel in New York. He went up to his room and ten minutes later came dashing down the stairs yelling, "Check me out, check me out!"

"What's wrong?" asked the excited man at the desk.

"I don't mind one cockroach; I don't mind two cockroaches," said the man, "but when I kill one cockroach and 1,800 come to the funeral, check me out!"

Opposition always inflames the enthusiast, never converts him.

Johann von Schiller

Never own defeat in a sacred cause.

Gandhi

Good humor makes all things tolerable.

Henry Ward Beecher

Mahomet made the people believe that he would call a hill to him, and from the top of it offer up his prayers for the observers of his law. The people assembled. Mahomet called the hill to come to him, again and again; and when the hill stood still he was never a whit abashed, but said, "If the hill will not come to Mahomet, Mahomet will go to the hill."

Francis Bacon—*Essays*

PARENTHOOD

An old couple was talking about the wonderful family of boys they'd had and the father was naming them over, mentioning their accomplishments. The mother was helping him remember.

"Bob, he was a doctor," the elderly gentleman said.

"Yeh, and there was Bill, he was out all night too," the lady added.

"Harry, he was a lawyer."

"Then, there was Gene, he never could tell the truth either."

"Lem, he was a preacher."

"Joe ended up in the poorhouse too."

"Raymond, he was a college professor."

"Yeh, and there was Zeke, he ended up in a state institution, too."

"Son, it's time we had a man-to-man talk."

"Okeh, Dad, what questions you got?"

A woman who had just had her sixth baby was looking rather displeased when the doctor arrived for his post-operative examination. "Why are you looking so glum; you have another beautiful child," said the doctor.

"I know, but my fifth child just graduated from high school."

"Well, what's wrong with that? You're still young."

"Yes, I know, but twelve more years in the P.T.A.!"

The successful man was lecturing to his son on thrift.

"My boy," he said, "when I was your age I carried water for a gang of bricklayers."

"I'm proud of you, Father," he said finally. "If it hadn't been for your work and thrift, I might have had to do something of the same sort myself."

Miss Huggins was having trouble with little Forney McShane, so she wrote his mother a letter:

"Your son is one of the brightest boys in my class, but he is full of mischief. What shall I do?"

The next day she received the following reply:

"Do as you please. I'm having my own troubles with his father."

PHILOSOPHY

To improve the golden moment of opportunity, and catch the good that is within our reach, is the great art of life.

Samuel Johnson

The humblest individual exerts some influence, either for good or evil, upon others.

Henry Ward Beecher

A pessimist is one who feels bad when he feels good for fear he'll feel worse when he feels better.

Anonymous

Safety Rules:
Stop accidents before they stop you.
With a moment of care a life you may spare.
Don't let recreation wreck your life. Know how to play safely.

The heavens themselves, the planets and this centre
Observe degree, priority, and place,
Insisture, course, proportion, season, form,
Office and custom, in all line of order.
William Shakespeare—*Troilus and Cressida*

You cannot stop a river from flowing—but you can divert it into other channels.

Wise men argue causes, and fools decide them.

Victor Hugo

POLITICS

Politics is the art of looking for trouble, finding it, whether it exists or not, diagnosing it wrongly, and applying the wrong remedy.

Sir Ernest Benn

I've got an acrobatic friend who's a politician. He can open his mouth, put his foot in it and stand on the fence all at the same time.

A politician from Fort Worth told an audience at a rally, "Some Texans brag a lot about how good they are, but I seldom brag about myself. In fact, I'm twice as good as I say I am."

During the last election, a constituent said to a candidate, "I wouldn't vote for you if you were Saint Peter."

The candidate replied, "You're right. If I were Saint Peter, you wouldn't be in my district."

A reporter asked Cal Coolidge how he felt about sex. He pondered the question for a moment then replied, "I'm in favor of it."

When a politician says that the nation is due for a reawakening, it means he is running for office.

The politician told one of his constituents, "I'm a self-made man."

"That's what I like about you," the voter replied, "always willing to take the blame for everything."

Politics divorced from religion has absolutely no meaning.

At three o'clock one morning, a constituent called the County Commissioner.

"I'm sorry if my call got you out of bed," the voter said.

"Oh, that's all right," the politician yawned, "I had to get up to answer the telephone anyhow."

George Washington could broad jump 23 feet. Quite a record in those days, but today we all know politicians who can side-step farther than that.

When Al Smith was running for Governor of the State of New York, he was presenting a campaign speech and one of his audience kitbitzed him unmercifully, "Go ahead and give your speech, Al," cried the man. "Tell us all you know. It won't take long."

"I will," said the late Governor, "I'll tell all we both know and it won't take any longer."

One of this book's authors sent a last-minute appeal to the voters on postal cards. The mimeographed message read:

"Be sure to go to the poles on November 10th and vote. Vote for Van Dusen for School Board."

A few days later, he received one of his cards back in an envelope along with a hastily scratched note which said:

"I intend to vote for Van Dusen on November 10th, but please tell me, should I go to the North Pole or the South Pole?"

PSYCHOLOGY

The business executive wanted to hire a new secretary and someone sold him on having a psychologist help him make his selection. The psychologist gave the applicants a simple test.

"How much is two and two?" he asked each of them.

"Four," answered the first.

"It could be 22," said the second.

"It all depends," replied the third.

The psychologist was satisfied with all three answers and he told the employer about the results and described the characteristics the answers revealed.

"So which one do you want to hire?" he asked, seriously.

The executive thought for a moment and said, "I'll take the blonde with the blue eyes."

A psychologist was giving a talk at an assembly of the inmates of the insane asylum.

"Why are we all here? Why . . . are we all here?"

During his dramatic pause, a voice came from the rear of the hall, "Because we ain't all there."

Ordinarily he is insane, but he has lucid moments when he is only stupid.

Heinrich Heine

The neurotic builds castles in the air; the psychotic lives in them; the psychiatrist collects the rent.

PUBLIC SPEAKING

A new preacher at the Wednesday night prayer meeting found that just one parishioner—a tall lanky farmer—had shown up for his sermon. He went down to the man and asked him if he thought he should give his sermon or dismiss the service. The man thought about it for a moment and said, "I ain't educated, but if I was to take a load of hay down to the pasture and only one cow comes up to git it, I'd feed her."

The minister decided he'd better give the talk. The man was a good listener and the preacher was in good voice and didn't have anything else to do that evening, so he went on for an hour and a half.

Afterwards, he went down to the man and asked him what he thought about the sermon. The farmer thought about it for a moment and then said, "I ain't educated, but if I was to take a load of hay to the pasture and only one cow comes up to git it, I'd feed her . . . but I'd be hanged if I'd give her the whole load."

The candidate for tax collector was delivering a campaign speech in the crowded hall when a fellow at the back of the room yelled, "Louder, louder! I can't hear a word you say."

A man down in the front row jumped up and said to the man at the back, "You say you can't hear a word he says?"

"That's right," came the voice, "I can't hear him."

"Fine," said the man down front. "I'll be glad to trade seats with you."

If you ever hear our speaker walking down the street talking to himself, it's because he likes to talk to a smart man. Also, he likes to hear a smart man talk.

A speaker opened his address by saying, "My subject is very broad. Like a mosquito at a nudist camp, I don't know where to start."

Mr. James had just been elected president of the country club and he was there pacing up and down as he practiced his speech.
A woman came in and asked him what he was doing there.
"I'm going to give a speech," he said.
"Do you get nervous when you are going to give a speech?" she asked.
"I should say not," he told her.
"Well," she said, "may I ask what you are doing in the ladies' room?"

Will everyone in the audience take a deep breath and say "Ah" as you sigh? All together now . . . Ahhh. That was fine. Now I feel important enough to stand up here and talk to this fine audience.

The best after-dinner speech I ever heard: "Waiter, I'll take the check."

After giving a fiery address, the speaker sat down.
"How did you like my execution?"
"Fine," his friend said, "I'm in favor of it."

I listened to the entire speech and finally reached one conclusion: the speaker was manufactured by the American Motor Company . . . a Rambler if I ever heard one.

RULES FOR PUBLIC SPEAKERS:

I appreciate that applause, but don't worry, I'm not going to tell another story! You know, one of the most needed devices in this country is some sort of a gauge that would enable an audience to tell just how much applause would make a performer feel good without being mistaken for an invitation to give an encore.

"I planned to present a phornographic film in connection with my lecture today," said the speaker, "but I couldn't find a phornograph."

A man was giving a speech before the inmates at an institution for the mentally unfortunate one day. They listened intently. No one moved from his seat except one man, who at about mid-point of the talk, got up, walked to the rear of the auditorium, said something in the ear of the guard, then walked out. After the speech was finished the speaker recalled the incident while talking to the guards. He turned to the guard who had let the man out and said, "By the way, what did that inmate who left the hall say as he went out?"

The guard thought for a moment and then replied, "All he said was that that was the longest and lousiest speech he had ever heard." The guard paused a moment then added thoughtfully, "You know, that is the most intelligent thing that man has said in years."

Stand up, speak up, shut up.

Tell 'em what you're gonna tell 'em; tell 'em; tell 'em what you told 'em.

Think yourself empty; read yourself full.

A speech should be like an artesian well. If you don't strike oil in three minutes, quit boring.

Be bright; be brief; be gone.

Drive home the point, not the audience.

REASON

Reason is the mistress and queen of all things.

Cicero

Men are apt to mistake the strength of their feeling for the strength of their argument. The heated mind resents the chill touch and relentless scrutiny of logic.

William Gladstone

Measure your mind's height by the shade it casts.

Robert Browning

Facts are stubborn things.

Tobias Smollett

An old resident of Cape Canaveral was permitted to watch researchers as they developed a new formula. He watched silently as the men went about their work. Finally, they finished and the project was successful. In his excitement one of the scientists walked over to the old man and bragged, "This new fluid will dissolve anything it touches and we're about to produce a million gallons."

The old gentleman took his pipe from his mouth, puffed some smoke into the air and said, "What are you going to keep it in?"

Clearness ornaments profound thoughts.

Vauvenargues

God has placed no limit to intellect.

Francis Bacon

RESPONSIBILITY

What you get out of life depends on choices you make. Steal: you go to jail. Work: you earn. Study: you learn.

A man asked the vice-president at the bank to give him just a little more time on his loan. The stern executive looked at him through his bifocals and said, "Your mother carried you for only nine months. Why should we carry you for twelve?"

A Scotsman, Irishman, and an Englishman attended a potluck picnic. The Irishman brought the drinks; the Englishman, the food, and the Scotsman brought his brother.

SELF-KNOWLEDGE

Myself: The person who gives me the most trouble.

A modest man never talks of himself.

La Bruyère

Allow yourself the extravagance of a dream.

We take ourselves entirely too seriously. The only thing we need to take seriously is whether we are contributing something to the world.

Kettering

SERVICEMEN

An English soldier was driving through the Adirondacks and suddenly noticed a sign at the top of a steep grade that read, "Drive slowly. This means you!"

"Wonderful country," mused the Limey. "How on earth did they know I was over here?"

An American soldier, standing outside Notre Dame Cathedral in Paris, saw a magnificent wedding procession enter.

"Who's the bridegroom?" he asked a Frenchman standing next to him.

"*Je ne sais pas*," was the reply.

A few minutes later, the soldier inspected the interior of the cathedral himself, and saw a coffin being carried down the aisle.

"Whose funeral?" he demanded of an attendant.

"*Je ne sais pas*," said the attendant.

"Holy mackerel," exclaimed the soldier. "He certainly didn't last long."

A librarian in Washington was stumped when a timid young serviceman asked for a book written by that eminent French author, Risqué.

At the beginning of World War II, a young fellow was inducted into the Army and appeared for his first physical examination. As the physician took out a pencil and the regulation form, the inductee said, "Hurry up, Doc! I want to get over there, get wounded, go to the hospital, get well, get out there on the battlefield again, get wounded, go back to the hospital, get well . . ."

"Son, you're crazy," the medic interrupted.

"Write that down!" said the soldier. "Write that down!"

SPEECH

Blessed is the man who, having nothing to say, abstains from giving in words evidence of the fact.

George Eliot—*Impressions of Theophrastus Such*

The party was over and the bachelor from next door said his

goodbyes and started to leave. The chatty host, who'd bent his ear most of the evening, said jokingly, "Can I drive you home?"

His prompt response was, "You have."

The tongue of the just is as choice silver: the heart of the wicked is little worth.

Proverbs 10:20

A wholesome tongue is a tree of life: but perverseness therein is a breach in the spirit.

Proverbs 15:4

An angry man opens his mouth and shuts up his eyes.

Cato

Birds are entangled by their feet and men by their tongues.

Thomas Fuller

That which is repeated too often becomes insipid and tedious.

Boileau

Speech is power: speech is to persuade, to convert, to compel.

Ralph Waldo Emerson

Rhetoric is the art of ruling the minds of men.

Plato

Speech is the index of the mind.

Seneca

A vessel is known by the sound, whether it be cracked or not; so men are proved, by their speech, whether they be wise or foolish.

Demosthenes

I must have small feet. They fit into my mouth so easily.

How forcible are right words!

Job 6:25

A stutterer had a difficult time telling the man in the ticket office that he wanted to purchase a one-way ticket to Chicago. Finally, in desperation, he said, "Hell, send me by freight. I can't express myself."

The voice teacher told her student, "We're going to work on pitch today."

"Great," the young fellow said, "when do we leave for the ball park?"

Lord, please fill my mouth with worthwhile stuff—and please nudge me, Lord, when I've said enough.

It is easier not to speak a word at all than to speak more words than we should.

Thomas à Kempis—*Imitation of Christ*

He was wont to speak plain and to the purpose.

William Shakespeare—*Much Ado About Nothing*

Originality does not consist in saying what no one has ever said before, but in saying exactly what you think yourself.

James Fitz-James Stephen

SPORTSMEN

A golfer had a strong drive, but he sliced the ball. One day, he stepped up and hit the ball and it went through the window of a nearby residence. He left his card and went on playing. His slice drove the ball through the windshield of a car that was parked near the golf course. He left his card and went on playing.

He slammed a drive and this time his ball struck a man in the temple and killed him. He left his card and went on playing. When the body was discovered the police were called. They followed him and when they reached him he was at the eleventh hole. "Look," the cop said, "you broke a window, a windshield, and now you've killed a man with your golf balls. What do you intend to do about it?"

"Well, I'll show you. I'm going to change my grip a little so I can get rid of that slice."

Rocky Marciano, the undefeated ex-heavyweight boxing champion of the world, was talking with Gypsy Rose Lee recently when the dancer asked, "What did you do just before going into the ring?"

Rocky replied, "I prayed. I prayed that everything would come off all right."

Gypsy said, "Me too."

Fisherman: "It was that long. . . . Never saw such a fish in my life."

Friend: "That, I can believe."

Two men went duck hunting. One of them carried a quart of milk to drink, the other a quart of whiskey. They got all set for ducks, but none flew over, so the one fellow drank his milk and the other his liquor. Just as they lifted their bottles for the last swallow a lone duck circled overhead. The milk drinker aimed his shotgun, fired and missed. The whiskey man aimed, fired and the duck fell a few feet away.

"You're handy with that shotgun," the milk drinker said.

"Oh, that was nothing," the whiskey drinker replied, "lotsa times I bring down two or three when I see a whole flock like that."

If athletes have Athlete's Foot, do astronauts have Missile Toes?

A man who was a well-known killjoy was described as a great athlete. He could throw a wet blanket two hundred yards in any gathering.

STUDENTS AND TEACHERS

The professor received a call late one evening from Ed Hale, one of his students. He'd missed his final examination and wanted a make-up. He offered the weak excuse that friends had arrived unexpectedly at the airport and he had to meet them. "Okeh, come to the office at nine in the morning," the professor said.

The boy didn't show at nine. In fact, he didn't get there till 9:40. When asked what had kept him, he said, "I been down on the ground floor, waiting."

"There are two elevators and two stairwells up to the third floor. Why didn't you come on up?" the professor asked.

"The elevators weren't working," the young man replied.

Ed was not permitted to take the exam, but he discovered a truth: Only sometimes is an elevator available. Quite often, it is necessary to walk up stairs to get a job done.

A teacher was called into the principal's office.

"I want you to teach Latin this semester," said the principal.

"But I've never taught Latin. In fact, I've never studied it."

"You like your job here, don't you?" the school head asked.

"Yes, sir, I certainly do," said the teacher.

"Then, teach Latin."

A week later, the class met for the first time. The teacher called the roll and then announced, "I have neither taught, nor made a thorough study of Latin." Then he reached down and picked up a book. "This is your textbook for this course. I am on lesson seven. Try to catch up."

A student was showing his grade report to his father . . . four "F"s, and one "D" in Algebra. The father puzzled, "How could you get all those 'F's?" The son responded, "I guess I concentrated too much on the math."

A teacher asked one of her students to tell the difference between unlawful and illegal.

"Unlawful, not according to law," said one young man.

"Illegal," came a voice from the rear of the room, "a sick bird."

After rigorous and regular exercises, the correspondence school student wrote to his teacher as follows:

"Dear Atlas:

Have just finished course. Please send muscles."

"Harold," the teacher said, "tell us what animals produce foods that humans eat."

Promptly he said, "Cows give us milk."

"Fine," said the teacher. "Can you name any others?"

"Horses give us meat."

The teacher swallowed hard and urged him to continue. He thought for awhile and finally said, "And camels give us soup."

The instructor told the student who was failing in his work, "You'd better give up wine, women and song." The instructor noticed a gradual improvement in the student's grades and he asked him if he had done as had been suggested earlier. The student replied, "Well, I gave up singing. Sure enough, my grades improved."

A hard-working senior was privileged to have her room on the first floor of her sorority house at Indiana University. She lived there for a month and, finally, asked the house mother if she might move to the third floor.

"But why do you want to move way up there? Those steps are murder," the older woman said.

"You're right about that," the coed said, "but only the good Lord would be above me. He's busy, but He's quiet."

In a science class at school, the teacher took out an angle worm and dropped it into a glass of water. It was happy and healthy when she took it out. She dropped it into glass of whiskey. After a few minutes, the worm died.

"Now what does that teach?" the teacher asked.

Without a moment's pause, one of the fellows in the second row said, "Drink whiskey and you'll never have worms."

SUCCESS

Success doesn't come to the sleeper.
Charles Capier—*Six Mille Proverbes*

The greatest orator in the world is success.
Napoleon Bonaparte—*Chigam*

By their fruits ye shall know them.
Matthew 7:20

Accomplishments are not accidents.
Kettering

"The president wants me to hire that bum, Harvey X. White," said the personnel officer. "What do you think?"

"Do it!" replied the business manager. "You can't argue with success. He picked us, didn't he?"

THEATRICAL JOKES

The two so-called "girls" went up to see the agent of R.C.A. Recording Company. "We would like to become recording artists," they said demurely.

"What experience have you had?"

"We used to sing for the army."

"Union or Confederate?"

As a composer I was always able to write verses easily but had trouble with the chorus . . . none of them would go out with me.

Why did I quit playing the flute in the pit at Radio City? Well, I'll tell you. One day I got sick and didn't show up for work. That evening the theater manager came down and complimented the orchestra on how much their music had improved. He even gave the bunch a raise. The fellows in the band were real happy. I never went back—just couldn't stand to see a nice bunch like that take a salary cut.

People talk about "light reading." I know what that is all right, but I've wondered about "dark reading." I guess that's what you do when you're trying to find out who's in the cast after the lights go out in the theater.

WEIGHT

A fat woman and a thin woman were sitting next to one another on a bus. Irked at having only half her seat, the thin woman said, "I think they should charge by weight, don't you?"
"If they did," said the fat woman, "they couldn't afford to stop for some people."

A boy from the country visited the city for the first time. He was walking down the main street when he came to an automatic weighing machine. He stepped to the scale, inserted a penny and got a little ticket. He looked at one side and noticed that his weight was 165 pounds. Then he turned it over and saw a picture of Rock Hudson. He turned to his friend and said, "It don't tell weight right, but it sure does take good pictures."

When asked how he kept his weight down, a man with a slim figure told his portly friend, "I touch my shoes twenty-five times every morning. Then I get up and put them on."

WIT

Avoid witticisms at the expense of others.

> Horace Mann

Neither irony nor sarcasm is argument.

> Rufus Choate

An adventurer took a trip into Mau Mau country where he was caught by the tribe. They tied him to a stake, piled around branches and lit the fire. A few moments later the man was heard to say, "I'm smoking more now but enjoying it less."

Brevity is the soul of wit.

> William Shakespeare

A joke loses everything when the joker laughs himself.

> Johann von Schiller

WOMEN

Two school superintendents were waiting on the platform for their train. One of the men wandered away and was later seen down by the freight office talking to two girls.

Later, when the men joined one another again, one asked,

"Who were those two girls I saw you talking to?"

The other replied, "I was interviewing them for jobs. They're teachers."

"Now, Bill, don't give me that. I could tell by looking at them that one had no principals and the other had no class."

Men who know tell us that the average woman has a vocabulary of only 500 words. A small stock, but think of the turnover.

A gentleman driving alone to Chicago picked up a beautiful blonde hitchhiker. When they became better acquainted the girl told the man, "I've great powers, I'm a witch."

"Aw . . . you're kidding. There's no such thing as a witch."

"Oh, yes there is," she insisted.

They drove on a little further and she put her arm around his shoulders.

"I really am a witch," she said, "I can turn a man into anything."

"Now don't give me that," he said, but she assured him.

They drove on a little further. She kissed him. And he turned into a motel.

When a woman has made up her mind, there is no power on earth that can keep her from changing it.

She didn't have much upstairs, but what a staircase!

At a banquet recently, a genial judge with an extra burden of avoirdupois didn't start to eat along with the others when he was served. A lady sitting next to him asked him why.

"I forgot my diet pills."

"Why not take a couple of mine?" the woman suggested, pulling a small bottle out of her purse.

"Okay . . . thanks," said the judge as he swallowed them down.

A man to his left asked, "Don't you want to know what kind of pill you're taking?"

"Yeh, what kind of pills were those?" he asked, turning to the lady.

"Female hormone," she answered.

WORK

You will look up to leaders—the people who become powerful through their own initiative. You may think they got appointed or elected, or they inherited their position. Often, this is not the case. Rather they saw a need for a thing and they took over. They have a knack for leadership. I can ask you to do a job, but if you don't take hold, the job doesn't get done. You're neither a worker nor a leader. Both are the same. A leader is a worker.

Work is like a game of tennis, if you serve well you win in the end.

A high school principal was trying to advise a difficult student on choosing a career. Finally the older man asked in despair: "Isn't there anything on earth you'd like to be?"

"Why, yes," the boy drawled, "I'd like to be a retired business-man."

Asked how he liked his work, a taxi driver in St. Louis told his passenger, "It ain't the work I enjoy, it's the people I run into."

The school superintendent visited a vice-principal in the hospital.

"Now, Bill," he said, "don't worry. Everybody at school will pitch in and do your work . . . as soon as we can figure out just what you've been doing."

The boss asked a north Florida boy, "Why are you going to quit? Are the wages too low?"

"No, the wages are okeh," the young man replied, "but I'm keeping a mule out of a job."

There is nothing better than that a man should rejoice in his own works.

Ecclesiastes 3:22

Do the best you can. The forests would be very quiet if all the birds were quiet except the best singers.

He is willing to try anything once, with the possible exception of work.

It takes more energy to complain about a chore that must be done than it does to go directly at it and have it out of the way.

INDEX